The Truth That LIES Within

Jonathan Marte'

The Truth That Lies Within

Copyright © 2017 by Jonathan Marte'

ISBN 978-0-692-04168-0 (paperback)

Library of Congress Control Number: 2019912916

Cover Illustration Copyright © 2017 by Jonathan Marte'

Cover Design by Jonathan Marte'

Book Design and Production by Jonathan Marte'

Editing by Gloria Josiah & Loretta Marte'

Illustration by Jonathan Marte'

Poetry by Jonathan Marte'

Photograph taken by Jonathan Marte'

Scripture taken from **The Hebrew-Greek Key Word Study Bible King James Version®**

Copyright © 1984, 1991 AMG International, Inc. Revised Edition 1991

Scripture quotations marked (KJV) are from the authorized King James Version

Printed in the United States of America

The Truth That Lies Within

Table of Contents

Dedication

God has shown me so much in a short period of time that all I want to do is say, "Thank You." The best thing one can experience in life is His wonderful grace and mercy. I don't have enough words to say, but I hope what is being said comes from the heart. I have come so far in my journey. Even though I am writing this book, I am not the true author. God has given me a new perspective on life and it must be shared. He is the true author.

Be of good courage, and he shall strengthen your heart, all ye that hope in the Lord (Psalm 31:24 KJV).

Acknowledgments

I would like to thank my mom and dad who have done so much for me. The best thing a mother can have is a child to love and to be loved. My mom exhibited characteristics during times of great difficulties, for which she should be commended. She has helped me tremendously. I will never understand a mother's love, but I have a good example, so thank you mom. My father and I have come a long way in our respective journeys and I have found that we have more in common than we first thought. I just want to acknowledge him as my father who has tried his best to live up to that as a parent. My parents may have their flaws, but one thing is clear among them both and that is their love for their children.

There are a few individuals who have been influential in helping me. Al and Collette Martin, Pastor John Josiah, Dr. Rambally Josiah, Chris Peters, Dr. Avonelle and Robert Dorant were all there to support, pray, and fellowship as I recovered what I had lost.

I would also like to thank my grand-father Freezell Brown, Jessica and Samuel Harris, and Bonnie Love for allowing me to stay in their homes.

I appreciate Gloria Josiah for editing the book and providing invaluable information on content.

To my brother Joseph Marte' for giving me advice and trying to cheer me up when I was at my lowest point.

I would like to express my gratitude towards Becky

Cash - ND Naturopath Doctor who taught me the values of living a healthy lifestyle and was involved in providing natural remedies while I was trying to heal.

Tim and Penny Surber thank you for coming to my aid when I needed you the most.

The connections I have made with individuals have taught me valuable lessons that go beyond a one word statement. The word family has been redefined for me and I will never forget the love and support of so many individuals. It is important not to forget the people who care about you. Thank you all.

Foreword

For the longest time my son has wanted me to contribute to this book. I kept putting him off with no answer. I wasn't sure that I wanted to be a part of it. I reasoned that it was his story and that he needed to tell it. But he would not have this story if his parents had not written the beginning for him. Children are a blessing. They are loaned to us from the Lord. It is our responsibility to love and protect them and give them back not tarnished by our bad decisions. There are enough negative things happening in this world that could possibly influence our children. We shouldn't let it happen in the home. The home should be a safe haven. I've seen my son go through a lot during the course of this journey. So many things. So many things not his fault. This book is about truth and lies and trying to determine which one a person is operating in. If we as adults look at the ills of the world carried out by our children and put the blame on them, we are living a lie. It doesn't matter the age, if needs are not met the way that they should be, because of our desire as human beings to live, it will be met in other ways.

Train up a child in the way that he should go; and when he is old, he will not depart from it. (Proverbs 22:6).

I had been living a lie. The first lie was that my husband would not do anything to my children. The second lie was that they would not be affected by their separation from me. As this book states sometimes the truth hurts a lot. I am tired of broken children because of broken adults. We don't choose our parents, but we do choose our children. Whether we want to look at ourselves or not it doesn't change the truth.

Preface

I find myself wondering, what is a lie and what is the truth these days? It seems to be all relative. As a Christian, I try now to know what is truth and its meaning. The Hebrew word for truth is Emeth which means firmness or to have stability. The best way to find truth is through the Word of God and His directions. The truth that lies within...

If I take the wings of the morning, and dwell in the uttermost parts of the sea; Even there shall thy hand lead me, and thy right hand shall hold me (Psalm 139: 9-10 KJV).

Black Willow ©2017 Jmarte'

Black Willow

How can this be?

While looking at this weeping tree

The void that was me

How can this be?

Where darkness enveloped me

Lost in the unseen

Feeling despondent of the past me

While staring at this black willow tree

I ask you, "How can this be?"

As I shrink

Not knowing where I would be

While looking at this black willow tree

I ran to the mercy seat

And asked the Father, "How can this be?"

The pain ran, so deep

As He is healing me from this black willow tree

Surrounded by shadowy beasts

By people who had hurt me

Never knowing what love truly means

Represented by this black willow tree

Asking myself, "Why me?"

Why did I have to go through these things?

Entangled and twisted

As I scream, "How can this be!?"

And groan for humanity

That looms over my very being

Through the depths of this dark willowy

As I grieve

I ran to the mercy seat

And asked our High Priest

To take away my black willow tree

Living inside of me

THE BEGINNING

FEBRUARY 2014: The beginning of my journey with God started off pretty rocky. I found myself in a situation where I was running away from nothing. The dreams I was having were disturbing, but they all had a common theme. My life was being threatened through my dreams. Satan was busy. I didn't know what to do, and during this time I did not trust in God either. I didn't even believe that He existed. All I knew was that I decided to exercise and run all the way to Cloverdale, IN, which wasn't easy. The run was not my idea, but nevertheless it was an experience I will never forget. The truth is that what I experienced during the run was based on a lie produced by Satan. I didn't know this during the time since everything was being produced by fear. God wanted to shake things up in my life and create a fruit that he could use to help others besides myself. The funny part of this experience was that I wasn't the only one who He decided to take on this journey. My mom decided to join me. She felt the need to protect me. Unlike me, she is a firm believer in the Father. She has many examples in her life of His presence. During this time of running, I heard a small voice asking me to be a disciple. I was overwhelmed by the thought only because I was involved in not so good things, and didn't think of myself as being worthy of such an honor. Later on, I embraced the idea thanks to some true believers, but it wasn't easy because I had lost touch with God for so long.

And whosoever doth not bear his cross, and come after me, cannot be my disciple (Luke 14:27 KJV).

After praying and talking to various people about this

situation, I found myself wondering what direction my life would take with God. The enemy wants me to stay silent about everything I have seen and experienced. Our greatest asset is our testimony. It is my desire that mine will be a blessing to others.

During my trial, I have learned to be thankful, and let patience have its' perfect work in dealing with it. I have lost almost everything but my faith. There isn't much a person can do when his back is up against the wall. I began to think, how could I be in this situation, "Why Me!?" But everything happens for a reason. My life before this situation didn't reflect what God wanted me to be both physically and spiritually. The truth or lies people create in their lives are beyond my understanding but not to God's.

He that walketh uprightly, and worketh righteousness, and speaketh the truth in his heart (Psalm 15:2 KJV).

The road that I was on previously was not the one that the Lord wanted me to travel. God needed to peel away the layers of my past so I could get to my true self. I wasn't living truth, but a lie, and it could have cost me more than I realized.

There are many people who are living a lie for reasons only God can understand. My desires were clouded by my colored past, like most people. Many of us have lost sight of what is truly important in life. People want to know what is truth, so their lives can be better. Developing a true belief system is a life long process, and does not come easy. LOOKING!?...I am. God can help manifest what is truth if we seek Him earnestly with our whole heart.

Behold, thou desirest truth in the inward parts: and in the hidden part thou shalt make me to know wisdom (Psalm 51:6 KJV).

Falsehood

Real...Fake

Nothing seems to be together

I know I'm here but am I

The more things move

The more things don't make sense

Strength becomes lost in the fray

Everything learned becomes frail and brittle

Move over to the side

It is a sense of false statements

Fostering what one can do to live

Me...You...They....We

They become superficial

Please let me become real

Chasing away what was left of me

Struggling to understand what went wrong

Pondering on what to do next

The next move

There...there...let it be real to me

DISCOVERING TRUTH

T o discover what is truth in one's life, the person must establish what lie he has been believing and then turn away from it or repent. Depending on the lie, this process can be easy to determine, or it may require a bit more work. Once it has been revealed, the person must make a conscious effort to live in truth, or face some type of consequence. This is the journey I am on.

I have chosen the way of truth: thy judgments have I laid before me (Psalm 119:30 KJV).

Nothing can be done within our own strength. Only through God can a person take the journey He has laid out for him. Facing a lie can be the hardest thing anyone can do. People are under stress these days for one reason or another; living their lives the best way they can. Some people are struggling financially, while others are battling some type of illness, having to make life changing decisions or face terrible consequences. Some people are blessed with abundance of riches, but are still not satisfied, wondering what's still missing in their lives. There are so many lies this world has created that it isn't funny. The things I have learned about this world has left me speechless. It is amazing that people these days have allowed this to continue for so long. Why?

I have found that anytime that a person puts his values upon the things of this world. They will ultimately be disappointed whether it be through status, material wealth or relationships. It is important to have realistic expectations. Nothing has a guarantee of success.

Success or failure is defined by the person and what truth or lie he believes. How do you define success? The meaning of this word does not have any set parameters that can be clearly define. It is up to the individual to interpret what success look like for them. Failure is a part of life. We are constantly being knocked down while struggling to live. Perseverance through life's challenges can often offer its own rewards one wouldn't expect. The thought of thinking of being a failure was overwhelming. I had fought many things in my life that has cultivated this way of thinking. This feeling of stupidity was a lie. It was foolish of me to believe, but I believed it. I was lost in thought thinking of those ugly words, "You are stupid!" Oh woe is me to those who are ignorant of the consequences of their words because they just don't know. Our words have power to uplift or tear down. Who are we to judge someone else intelligence?

How do you define intelligence? You can't. A person can be knowledgeable in one area of his surroundings while another individual maybe completely ignorant. It is all base on the environment the person is accustom too. For example, it is like a fish who freely swims in water, but when it is put on dry land it doesn't have a clue on what to do. Humans are more sophisticated than a fish by being able to adapt with the soul purpose of survival. You can't put a label on intelligence. Each one of us are uniquely and wonderfully made. We all interpret the world differently. The source of what you believe will drive how you gauge yourself in relation to someone else. Stop comparing your inadequacy or strengths with others. You are special. People reinvent themselves all the time, while in the process of trying to filter their emotions. But the reality of it is that a rich man may feel poor, but a poor man may feel rich.

People are doing their best to live their lives out in truth or in a lie. The question is which one? This kind of answer can only be determined by the decision making of the individuals. We are living in a world based on truth and/or lies. This belief system has been developed since the time we came from our mothers' wombs. Lies can be generated by a multitude of negative emotions. Identifying where these emotions originated is important and can determine how our viewpoint is affected. When someone believes a lie, he forms reasons or "connectors" to the lie. Sometimes a person can form these connectors to the point where he is blaming someone else instead of getting to the root of the lie. The truth is that lies hold problems, truth holds solutions. Once the person realizes this he can form solutions, or come to a resolution of whatever he is thinking to be truth. No decision making comes from nothing. It either comes from something we have learned, or something we believe. We learn certain things as an act of survival. We believe things hoping that the outcome will work in our favor. This concept is interchangeable, because what we learn eventually becomes part of what we believe. You are of what you believe. After realizing this for myself I came to the conclusion that the Lord would be my Great Director. We all experience truth and lies everyday, it does not discriminate between those of us who are living. It is my hope that this experience will have a positive impact on my life and others. During my deliverance process I was constantly asking the Father in prayer to guide me and to *"Order My Steps,"* Artist: by Gmva Woman of Worship.

Here are the steps I utilized for my own introspection.

Formula of Introspection

1.) *Ask God to search out your heart*

1. Reveal what has been seen and/or hidden*
2. Humble yourself*
3. Open up your heart*
4. **Be honest with Him and yourself***

2.) <u>Realize You Are Not Alone*</u>
3.) <u>Look deep within yourself</u> *

1. Ask yourself how has this influenced me?
    1. How has the truth and/or lies affected you in your everyday life?
2. Examine your own perception of reality
    1. What do you perceive from your inner and/or outer world?
3. Understanding your own perspective
    1. How do you view yourself or someone else?
4. Reflect on what you like or don't like about yourself or someone else

4.) Examine or reexamine your motives
5.) Acknowledge the truth and/or lie(s)

1. Type out your truth and/or lies
2. Think about the source of your beliefs

6.) Forgive yourself and/or someone else **(It Takes Time)***

1. Adopt an attitude of gratitude **(Be Thankful)**
2. **<u>Let go of...(Negative Emotions/Positive)*</u>**
    1. **<u>Red Font/Black Font</u>**
    2. False Self-Image **(Lies)**/ Authentic **(Truth)**
    3. Shame/Self-Compassion
    4. Stress/Relax
    5. Anxiety/Faith
    6. Regret/Grateful
    7. Resentment/Merciful
    8. Confusion/Clarity
    9. Guilt/Innocent
    10. Frustration/Patience
    11. Bitterness/Peace
    12. Pride/Humility
    13. Fear/Courage
    14. Betrayal/Loyalty
    15. Rejection/Acceptance
    16. Discouragement/Encouragement

17. Envy/Kindness
18. Blame/Accountability**(yourself or someone else)***
19. Disappointment(s)/Achiever
20. Revenge/Forgiveness
21. Sadness/Grief/Happiness
22. Depress/Hope
23. Loneliness/Friendship
24. Anger/Hatred/Love

7.) Have realistic expectations

8.) Take accountability of what you have done, said, felt, or believed
1. Understand that there are good and bad consequences and habits

9.) Listen to yourself (or your emotions)
1. What am I feeling?
    1. Identify your emotions and connect them to the truth and/or lies
    2. Remain grounded with your emotions
2. Why am I feeling this way?
3. How can I move pass this event or emotion(s)?
4. Who do I need to talk to? **(subjectively*)**
5. When did I start to feel this way?
6. What can I do constructively to address this issue(s)?

10.) Learn from addressing the issue(s) (internally or externally)

11.) Accept and/or Deny **(Truth and/or Lies)**

12.) ***<u>Type out a conclusion summary</u>***
1. State what you have learn from the process
2. State what you need to work on in regards to the truth and/or lies

Here is the process when using the formula...

<u>**Process of Introspection**</u>

[Subject]

Truth

Make a list in bullet point format

Lies (Type In Red Font)

Make a list in bullet point format **(Type In Red Font)**

Conclusion Summary

Please use "I" statements when utilizing this exercise. Also use who, what, when, where, why, and/or how to illustrate where you need to identify the issues. The purpose of the process of introspection is for both, or one side(s) to try and understand themselves connected to their issue(s). If there are two or more parties involved in the process of introspection, there will be some similarities and differences in regards to how each side feels and represents themselves to each other.

These emotions are spiritual like beings that are manifested in our physical bodies, and can stem from what we believe to be...truth and/or lies. We are spiritual beings living in a natural existence in this physical world. How do we draw the line between these two worlds of natural and spiritual? How do we draw the line between truth and/or lies? Try your best to answer these questions for yourself. What do you truly believe?

My emotions during the time were all over the place because of circumstances beyond my control. I could not tell who was friend or foe and was in a state of confusion. My family was doing their best to try and help me, but they too also looked like the enemy. I wasn't completely sure what the cause of my condition, I could not tell what was truth and a lie. I went for another run that could have placed my life in jeopardy. I ended up in the hospital thanks to the medicine I was taking and because of other factors. Later on I was diagnosed with schizophrenia. My first thought was *what is schizophrenia?* I had encountered many terminologies in my lifetime, but I wasn't familiar with this one. No one told me what I was dealing with which left me scared and confused. After looking up the information myself my heart dropped. I didn't want to believe it. Schizophrenia is a brain disease that causes hallucinations, delusions, and unusual speech patterns that could lead to a psychotic event. I had been through so much in my life and now I have to deal with this. The world I once knew has changed, but yet it remains the same. I have learned so much from this situation about the world, I wish the circumstances were different.

Buy the truth, and sell it not; also wisdom, and instruction, and understanding (Proverb 23:23 KJV).

The system is first created by the parents and those values are passed down to the child. As the child matures, it learns certain things that can be helpful or harmful in its development as an individual. Unfortunately, children are exposed to two different thought processes, the parents' views, and the world's views. The opposite effect is also true when it comes to the structure, or belief system of any particular household. The child could be expose to one type of thought process where the worlds views are in line with the parents views. This subject is somewhat elusive only because not all things are agreed by the parent(s), nor the world. This type of confusion can come in many forms depending on the child's experiences, physical disposition, and environment. Parents need to spend time with their children by teaching them good values that will carry them over to adulthood. The child needs to have opportunities to formulate his own sense of identity. I have learned that proper communication both in and outside of the home is important to the child as well as the parent(s). When a parent communicates, the child interprets the adult's motives and reacts in a positive or negative response depending on the situation and other experiences. The connections that are formed within the family can be different from child, parents, and grandparents. Even though there are connections that were previously molded, for whatever reason, those relationships in families have not been defined completely. The family structure remains the same across the board not improving, but not deteriorating. Hopefully these associations are motivated with real, genuine intentions. Human interaction is very important especially to a child's social development. Technology has formed a disconnect when it comes to human interactions and children are exposed to this disconnect at an early age. This is why it is important to physically spend time with your children. I know that can be difficult, because parents are busy with other responsibilities. What I have learned when it comes to parenting children through my own experiences as a child is that, it is important to be honest to yourself as well as the child. Parents with issues that they have not dealt with can be blind to how they teach their children. Please try to understand, the times you spend with your children are fleeting, but the memories that are formed last longer. Time itself represents the past, present, and future where everything moves forward but not backwards. This is not how memories operate. Memories last longer than time itself. Children and parent(s) remember the good and bad times. Hold on to the good memories and don't let go. Share those moments with each other and learn what it means to truly love one another. Children are doing there best to try and make it in this world. It is not easy for them to established a true relationship with their parent(s). Should a child have to earn their parent's love and affections? Unfortunately, there are children out there who are doing that very thing. The child begins to think negatively about themselves until they act out their feelings. They keep a running tally of all the things they have not received emotionally. What the child seeks is love and understanding. What type of future do you want for your child?

Do you want to be a part of it? Why did you decide to have children? They are life breathing beings who looked to their parents for a hug, a kiss, or to hear, "You did good job." It is not something parents should take lightly. The child didn't asked to be brought into this world to experience things like hatred, anger, loneliness, or despair. Unfortunately, there are so many broken homes in our country. Single parents and children are crying out, "Help!" I ask you, *"What About The Children,"* Artist: Yolanda Adam?

And, ye fathers, provoke not your children to wrath: but bring them up in the nurture and admonition of the Lord (Ephesian 6:4 KJV).

People lie to themselves everyday about things they don't want to face or have not accepted the truth. What lie have you been believing? Internalizing everything does not lead to a truth. I can sympathize. You feel like no one will be able to understand what you maybe going through, but that is not true. While I was internalizing my emotions, I would have flashbacks to trouble times in my past. These black and white images would be so vivid that I didn't know what to do. These colorless moments long forgotten were locked in my own psyche. I felt shackled by these events. The walls were closing in until I would panic. I would take slow and deep breath that would be difficult to manage. My heart would beat uncontrollably. Time would seem to move more slowly as I relived the actions of my oppressors. My surroundings became a blur and sounds were distorted. My body would be quivering begging for relief. I would desperately try to find someone to share my feelings. But I was too afraid to get close to anyone. I was in a dismal state. My defenses were up and I didn't want to let anyone in. I sealed my heart to everyone and everything. It was my last resort. I was carrying a heavy burden and didn't know what to do. It is during this time where the lie overwhelmed me as I was responding to the pain. It drained me. As troubling as the events were, I now know that the Lord was carrying me through it all as an injured little lamb. He is true to his word. He is the Good Shepherd. I am still being carried today. Unlike our ability to do so, the Lord is ever present. I can't express to you what His love means to me. I still have some growing to do since I alienated myself from people. Social situations had become a challenge. I am currently learning what it means to have boundaries. I didn't know how to handle different personas of individuals. I felt attacked believing I needed to defend myself. I thought that it was useless to express my feelings. But that was a lie. Interpersonal communication takes time to master, especially when interactions are being precipitated by events leading towards a confrontation. You have a voice and the power to do something about it in a constructive way. I know it can be difficult when dealing with negative influences in your environment.

Succumbing to peer pressure, or intimidation can often be devastating to a person. We all know that it is not right to bully, but yet why do people do it? Why do people take pleasure in deliberately hurting others feelings? Babies are not born into this world as bullies. I have been bullied myself, so I know how it feels. You are probably feeling that there is nothing you can do to appease the situation. You feel trapped. There are always options if people are willing to step back and examine their circumstances. You know what you are feeling, so do something about it. Stop looking for others to validate your existence. You are special. All you need to do is believe it. The true story of your life must be told. A unique narrative written by you daily. You are in control. Your life's tale doesn't end with you. The connections that you have made helps define who you are, but not who you ought to be. We are all connected to each other in some way. When you know who are in Christ your thoughts and actions are not your own. The Lord knows what you have gone through. The meaning of your existence is within each of us. We are precious gifts with untapped potential waiting to be opened. It is up to us whether we want to receive it. My mom said something to me that I didn't realize. It was really profound.

She said, "Do you understand the pain you were causing the Lord?"

I had to paused for a second. I didn't think about that. All I was thinking about was the pain I went through in my life. I had plenty to be thankful for, but that didn't cross my mind. I had no words to say. I had been complaining about my experience instead of being grateful. We sometimes can take things for granted, especially when we are angry about something. After brewing over my own issues, I felt empty inside as though a part of me was missing. I didn't know who I was anymore and had lost sight of myself. Do you know who are? It got to the point where I got tired of crying. The emptiness inside was growing. I continued doing things that I thought would bring me happiness. Ask yourself this question. What void are you trying to fill?

This maybe your responds, "I have suffered so much. How can I move forward? I have so many questions and very few answers."

That is alright. It is okay not to have all the answers. Don't feel ashamed or afraid about asking for help. No one is pressuring you. This is a time for you to grow and used your experience in a positive way. It is important to know your emotional threshold and communicate your problems with someone you can trust. What truth have you been believing? A person can sincerely think he has formed a truth based on a lie, which is not good. This type of lie can be dangerous depending on the subject matter because the person can take extreme measures to do something harmful or destructive to themselves and others. Depending on what the person believes can determine his or her own destiny, but that too is also relative. One man's lie is another man's truth. In our world one cannot exist without the other and are synonymous.

And they bend their tongues like their bow for lies: but they are not valiant for the truth upon the earth for they proceed from evil to evil, and they know not me, saith the Lord (Jeremiah 9:3 KJV).

When people make decisions in life, they are motivated by something they believe. Actions or comments committed by others form the bases for a truth or a lie. Circumstances in one's life can dictate his actions. This can be damaging, especially if he doesn't believe in God. Without knowing God, how can you come to a state of healing? Comments are powerful and can have the potential to have long term effects on a person's self worth. It is a sad prospect when one truly has lost something so valuable as their inner self. For some, this leads them to think of themselves as being common or unwanted. Many people have inferiority complexes. They are intimidated by anyone that they deem to be more intelligent than they are. If a person looks closely while going through a trial there are blessings on, *"The Other Side of Through,"* Artist: by James Bignon and Deliverance Mass Choir.

While I was being delivered, I was asked a question by a friend who was trying to help me. "What do you want?" My response was, "I want to be healed." During this time I was going through emotional and spiritual crises. I was feeling things happening to my body that would be deemed abnormal. After the person asked me that question, I began to wonder the meaning to the word deliverance and came up with an analogy. I call it, "The Baby and The Gold Piece." There once was a baby who came across a piece of gold and started playing with it. The baby could only see how hard and shiny the piece of gold is, but has not realize the value of the piece. Later on I told this analogy to my friend. How could I know what deliverance is if I don't understand it? Afterwards, I went back to studying the Bible to find the answer.

*And said, Verily I say unto you, Except ye be converted
and become as little children, ye shall not enter into the
kingdom of heaven (Matthew 18:3 KJV).*

*Whosoever therefore shall humble himself as this little
child, the same is greater in the kingdom of heaven (Matthew
18:4 KJV).*

*And whoso shall receive one such little child in my
name receiveth me (Matthew 18:5 KJV).*

Humbling myself as a little child did not come easy
because I was holding on to a lot of issues; which included a
lack of forgiveness. I felt then like a newborn babe in the eyes
of the Father.

*Wherefore laying aside all malice, and all guile, and
hypocrisies, and envies, and all evil speaking (1 Peter 2:1
KJV).*

As newborn babes, desire the sincere milk of the word,

that ye may grow thereby (1 Peter 2:2 KJV).

If so be ye have tasted that the Lord is gracious (1 Peter 2:3 KJV).

There are verses in the Bible that illustrate the need to forgive others.

Jesus saith unto him, I say not unto thee, until seven times: but, until seventy times seven (Matthew 18:23 KJV).

It took me a while, but I finally figured out what deliverance meant. The meaning of the word deliverance is to be set free from whatever was holding you bondage. Freedom is its purpose and the only one who can set you free is Jesus Christ. Humbling yourself is the first step and recognizing that whatever lie dwells within can be overcome. Trust God to handle the situation and be honest with Him and yourself. Honesty in any relationship is important. Allow God to melt your heart and seek answers from Him. I know it can be difficult to understand in the beginning. The road to deliverance can be short, or long, but it can happen if you have faith and put your trust in Jesus Christ. I am speaking from experience that once you have Christ, your life will never be the same. The important thing is that you are alive. There is always a chance to be hopeful and each day brings about a new beginning. There is also an opportunity to rectify or correct wrong doing and start fresh. *"Deliverance is Available,"* Artist: Vicky Yohe.

My Child

Children of light

Come to me with your plight

For I know what is right

From everlasting to everlasting

For I am Christ

The one who can handle all things in your life

I knew what you would be

Before you knew me

Son...Daughter...Mother...Father

All were ordain by me

For what you see and believe

Will manifest through me

For I am the vine and you are the branch

Never forget that Jonathan

Your need of me

TALES OF A BROKEN VESSEL

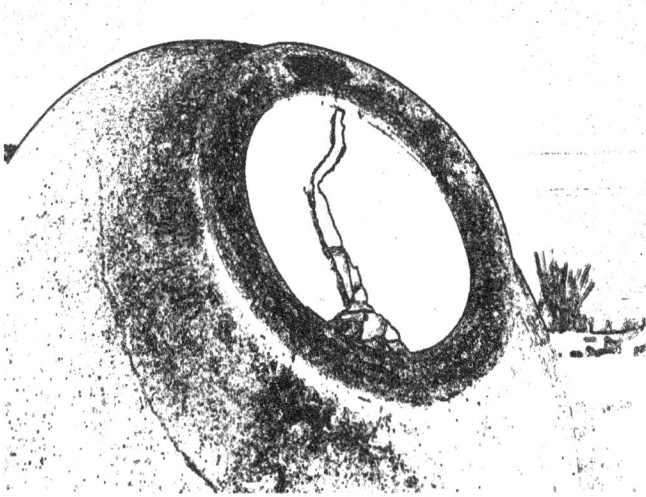

W ell, where to begin? I never thought I would be writing and sharing this with you. Life was extremely difficult for me. It isn't easy for me to talk about, but I feel like it is necessary for you to understand my back story. I am one of three children. I have a twin brother name Joseph and a older sister name Jessica. All three of us have experienced trauma during our childhood. We were born and raised in the city of Indianapolis, Indiana and this is where my story begins.

After going through repeated crisis from our father Ruben, my mother had enough. She took us away from him and brought us to our grandparent's house. It wasn't the first time we left my father, but this time was different. I was too little to understand what was going on between my parents. The little bit I do remember from that time are fragmented. There were a few times where the police were called, and I remembered them taking my father away. One of the events involved a fight between my uncle and my father inside the apartment. My uncle went crashing into my sister's bicycle and people were screaming, or my mother crying in the bathroom in the dark and me wondering why? I was at least two years old when all these events took placed. These were turbulent times for me and my family.

It was during this time that things went from bad to worst. The day my mother left and took us away from him for a final time was the day that my father paid us a visit to my grandparent's house demanding the custody of us. All of my relatives were present. I was busy taking a nap when all of this was going on. It was during this time that my mother had to make a decision and she had to choose between letting him take us, or her keeping us. My sister was the only one old enough to refuse his demands. During this time, I did not understand why my mother made the decision to let my father take my brother and I, but it would come to haunt me for next twenty-five years of my life. I remembered waking up being back at the apartment confused and wondering where is my mommy?

After my father took me, he went back to my grandparent's house and asked my grandmother to watch us while he went to work. She agreed to do it. My mother was furious and confused as to why my grandmother would make such a decision. She explained to her that if she did not agreed to do it we will never see them again. It was a hard choice for everyone involved. I did not fully understand why my father was keeping us away from my mother. I would have moments in time where I would see her comeback to my grandmother's house, but it would be short lived. My father would make sure to pick us up on time. It was torture for me and my mother.

During this time, the separation from my mother had

some negative effects on me. I was showing signs of depression and did not even realized it. I would go to use the bathroom and would not even clean myself. My underwear would be so soiled; I felt dirty and unclean. The problem would persist even after I entered into my first year of school.

Capital City

I grew up going to church on Saturdays in a denomination known as Seventh-Day Adventist. The people were nice to me and my family for the most part. Saying things like, "Happy Sabbath!" Little did I know that there was a dark side brewing in the Seventh-Day Adventist faith. There were many instances of domestic violence, child abuse, and bullying in the church. In regards to my situation, the church knew about the abuse my father was inflicting on his family and most did nothing about it. I was really angry with the church for a long time for not helping us. It was also the place where I saw my mother, but could not go to her for unknown reasons. During children church I would see her and whispered, "Hi Mom." After it was over, I would slipped towards the pew where she was sitting and sat with her during the service. After the service was over, I would look for my father only to find out later on that he had left me. I would start crying wondering, "Where is daddy!?" I was so confused. My mom would picked me up and take me back to my grandparent's house. It didn't matter at that point for me because I was with my mommy, but it was short lived.

When we arrived at my grandparent's house my grandmother would be surprised to see me, and would questioned how I had managed to sneak away with mommy. My mother would explain to her what had happened and my grandma would just smile. Not too long after that conversation, the phone would ring and it would be my twin brother. I don't really remember our conversation, but it was enough for my mother to make another mistake and I would end up back with my father. The reason why she took me back was because she did not want me to be separated from my twin brother. But from my vantage point she abandon me. This pattern of feeling emotionally abandon continues to this day. I have many issues because of those events. A decision we would both regret. My mother loves me, right? But...I...just don't know anymore.

What does love look like to me? I feel as though I am plucking away a daisy just to see where that last petal will fall. Will it fall on truth or a lie? She loves me. She loves me not. I would sometimes stare out of the window towards the heavens wondering what she would be doing at that very moment. After speaking with my mom and coming to a realization of how my sister, my brother, and I have interacted with her. I have come to realize that we have been competing for her attention, while at the same time taking advantage of her because of our own issues caused by the separation. I just want to say, "I am sorry mom." She shared with me how hard the separation was and she cried herself to sleep for years. She realized the effects of the separation and tried to compensated in financial ways. She even allowed us to disrespect her. She shared with me about how we all were separated. Even though my sister was with her, because so many thing continued to happen, it was like they were not really together. There were many things she wanted to teach my sister, but her focus kept getting diverted. She let me know that she wasn't completely absent from my sister's life, but enough to appear as if they were not really in the house together. My mom is very sorry. She hope one day her children will be able to forgive her and I do forgive my mother. My relationship with my family has been strained thanks to my father.

I don't really have a good relationship with my brother Joseph only because my father did not fostered that relationship between the two of us. We would fight often and sometimes my father would join in on the confrontation. I would get double team on a regular bases. There were a few moments where our fights almost went too far. Sometimes, it would take all my strength to get my brother to stop fighting me. The loneliness inside was growing over the years.

My sister Jessica and I have been separated for a long time. I have tried to get close to her, but she always keeps me at arms length. I try my best to hold on to the things I do know about her that are good, but it isn't easy. Like the time she protected me from Joseph and my dad.

This process of going with my mom would repeat itself a couple of times, but deep down I never really wanted to be with my father in the first place. After years of reexamining those events, I realized that my brother was not even old enough to use a phone, so how did he get to talk to me? I realized later on how calculated my father was during those times.

There are good and bad people everywhere regardless of their faith or belief system. The church was no exception to the rule. They needed help addressing some of these issues. This is about sharing what I know and hopefully something good will come from it.

I was so excited to be in the first grade and attend my first day of school at Capital City. Unfortunately, it was short lived. I struggled for a longtime with understanding my lessons. I did not even start reading fluently until I was about nine years old. But that was not the only issue I had during my schooling. I was being bullied by the kids at Capital City and abused by my father as well. I had no peace at school nor did I have it at home.

I would get screamed at for every little mistake I would make. It was during this time I was asking my father for help with my schooling. I had no one to run too. There were even times where I went into the school crying because of what my father had said to me. It wasn't until I was in the fifth grade that I had made the decision to stop asking my father for help with my schooling.

The abuse lasted for fifteen years and the bullying was about twelve years. I experienced everything from physical confrontations, emotional distressed, and psychological abuse. I was even sexually harassed by my peers. I had no friends and my trust to allow anyone to get close to me was torn to shreds. I was in survival mode most of the time. I would play by myself and not talk to anyone. All for the sake of maintaining some level of sanity.

In order to fight the loneliness I begged my father to buy me a pet, so I would have someone to play with when I was alone. I wanted a dog, but I could not get one since we lived in a apartment, so he bought me a cat. I named her Jasper, but most of the time I would call her Kitty.

The Final Straw

The final straw for me happened during my sophomore year of high school. My father took us out to eat right before school started and I was sitting in the front seat with him. I did not like sitting next to him and would try my best to avoid it. My father figured out what I was doing and started mandating days where my brother and I were forced to sit in the front seat with him. When he started yelling at me stating that, "You need me!" and that "You are nothing without me!" I stormed out of his SUV and proceeded to walk all the way from 86th street and Michigan Road to my high school North Central. My father tried to follow me, but I kept walking. Eventually, he drove off and I was finally alone walking towards the school carrying my backpack filled with books and a bunch of 2x4s from my wood shop class. After the incident, the tension in the apartment was extremely high and my grades in school suffered as a result. I tried my best to not make eye contact with him. My father did not say a word to me. I tried to leave him again only this time I was planning on walking to my grandparent's house, but he stopped me.

It wasn't until my mother finally gain custody of us that things got better for me in school. I was finally happy, but there was still some issues within me. I was even hiding some of these issues from my mother because I felt ashamed, bitter, angry, and alone. I was emotionally crying out for help in more ways than one.

EMOTIONAL OUT CRY

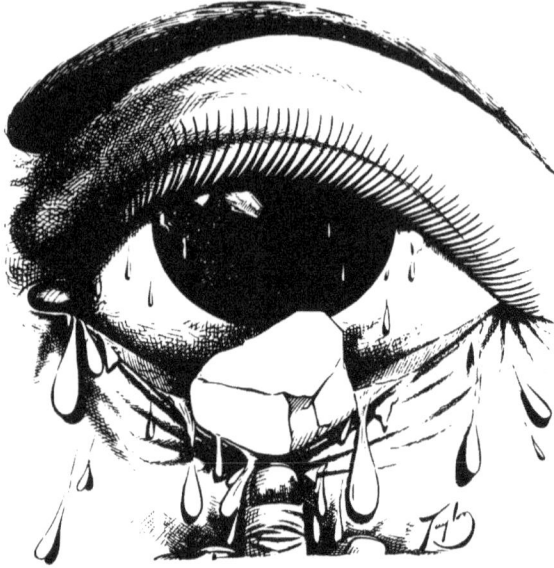

As I was in a peaceful sleep, chaos ensued at the age of three. It was the beginning of my journey. I cried out for the one who nurtured me only she didn't answer. I was taken by a man who was blinded by his own lie. I was awakened wondering what had happened. The man who I grew to despise and rejected for this act. It was not fair to be separated from my mother or to hate my father. I had lost both of my parents on that day. I walked this road never traveled not by choice. The feelings I once had of joy and happiness were taken away from me. Asking myself why me...why me? I felt alone and scared. The events that followed had me in a bind. My emotions were all over the place not realizing the state of my inner being. After going through years of repeated crisis from without and within, my spirit was broken into a million pieces. I blamed my mother and was angry with my father. I am currently trying to let go the pains of the past. It isn't easy. I was crying out and didn't know what to do. Forgiveness was the last thing on my mind but I had forgiven them.

Not being able to forgive doesn't benefit anyone spiritually, emotionally or physically. All it does is bring about resentment and bitterness. When a person is influenced by a lie at an early age, it is difficult for them to see anything else. Circumstances surrounding people cause them to have tunnel vision clouding their perception of reality. Try to understand your perspective. Everything is not always what it appears to be during times of peace or unrest. I can sympathize with those who are overwhelmed by intense negative emotions caused by events in their past. I too, have issues forgiving people even after they have apologized. The events run through my head like an awful infomercial. I plead with you, let go of the hurt and forgive the person. You will gain nothing by holding on to the pain. I felt the same way in my own despair. You are not alone. The feelings of loneliness and anguish are things I am familiar with. It is like drinking poison through the venom of your past or being constricted to the point of suffocation. These poisonous thoughts, or behavior are laced in a sea of chaotic emotions and events caused by the toxicity of your heart. Please I beg you let go of these toxic emotions. Your feelings are justified, but being sorrowful will only go so far and in the wrong direction. It is like swinging on a playground alone. Creak...Squeak...Creak...the sound of a lonely swing, blowing in the wind, dangling, being held up by rusty screws. You are defiant until the bitter end. As the heavens open, you cry and become overwhelmed by feelings of familiarity. While other times, you felt as cold as a blacken frost, but today it is windy. The leaves rustle in the background. You hear the noise from the void. The howling voice of seasons past. What is a throne if there is no one to sit in it? Is it nothing more than an empty space that needs to be filled? Is your purpose being fulfilled?

You need to be honest with yourself. What can you do? I need you to, *"Forgive Me"* Artist: by Anthony Evans.

Counting The Seasons

There is a season

A change in the air

As settle as the dew drops

The mist left by a summer rain

Steaming of what was in the purest of hearts

There is a piece of stone chipped away

What was left grew numb

Cold Hearten

The season of autumn dusk has begun

Be of good cheer

Change will come

The leaves will fall

A new season has begun

As the days grow shorter

Stormy winter chill set in

Now is not the time to run

Where can anyone go being surrounded by what is white

Pale as the rose on a rosy cheek

There I can see how deep

The lost of what made you unique

As this season begins a new

It will end with you

Only to have it start over again

Spring...Summer...Fall....Winter

Count the moments and days a loft

As I work closer

My time will come

Wait patiently everything will happen in due season. Please realize the emotional wounds you've carried can be healed, don't be confounded by what I'm saying. You deserve to be happy. We are creatures of emotions with various range of feelings that influences us on a regular bases. How we react to those feelings is directly related to what we believe about ourselves and the world. On the road to forgiveness confrontation is the most difficult thing to address. It is inevitable to have disagreements with people. Face to face conversations tend to be the most beneficial. It is how we respond in those difficult moments that test our resolve and allows us to grow from the experience.

It is best to go into the conversation with no expectations. During the encounter, try not to take things personal. The objective is to communicate your feelings, not to aggravate things by provoking the person. Realize, this is about you not the other individual. If you are going to have issues dealing with the lie, then you will need to handle the situation differently. Ask God to reveal what needs to be done in order for you to move forward. My journey has compelled me to assist those whose lives have been plagued by lies.

It is my goal to help others that have been holding on to something erroneous, a lie, and help them see their true self. There are many individuals trapped in their own lie. Why...why do people believe in lies instead of truth? Lies seem to be more attractive to people than the truth. I can't say I like that scenario. People make justification with their decisions when it comes to living a lie. It takes more work to cover up a lie and sometimes more people. There's also more stress involved with lies. You are constantly worried that the truth will come out. This is why it is important to know who you are in the Father and to try your best to live your life in truth. Also, some people may find that living a lie is more comfortable. For the truth maybe too painful for them to face. It is best not to look at

45

another person's window wanting what they have, and to *"Be Grateful,"* Artist: by Walter Hawkins.

The prince that wanteth understanding is also a great oppressor: but he that hateth covetousness shall prolong his days (Proverbs 28:16 KJV).

Life can be a great teacher; it has many insights, challenges, and rewards if the person knows where to look. I know one area of life that doesn't lie, and that is your body. One morning I felt weird. I didn't understand what was going on with my body. All I knew was that my face and arm were hurting me. My body had been under a lot stress and for some reason I felt really tired. I had been doing positive things like reading my Bible, writing in my journal, and listening to gospel music. I guess the things I was doing have been a benefit for my body. The only thing I could think of is that my body had been under emotional trauma and was releasing stress at different places.

Peace I leave with you, my peace I give unto you: not as the world giveth, give I unto you. Let not your heart be troubled, neither let it be a afraid (John 14:27 KJV).

I have been under some stress thanks to the situation, but I know my heavenly Father is in control. God doesn't want me to be afraid. Fear...can be a powerful emotion, but God will replace it with peace. Stress can be a component when it comes to clouding truth. People these days are living with broken hearts for one reason or another and are in need of, *"Healing,"* Artist: by Kelly Price.

The Locket

Bound together by soulless beings

Are two minds, one heart; one hand of fate

Never did they learn how to embrace

The embodiment of the locket

Nor took solace in their own love

While embracing their heart's desires

As they bear the markings of the locket

And gaze through the eyes of the new moon

With palms sweating, hearts racing

Words stumbling for sense of meaning

For this is the tragic love song of fate

That's filled with the aroma of human intuition

And the embodiment of two kindred spirits

That embraces the love song of the heavens

Through the mysteries of the Rosetta Stone

That's steeped in the pool of crimson blood

And reaps the soul of scarlet roses

Through the corpse of human remains

Are the limbs of my beloveth

That grows in the stem of every rose

And seeps throughout my mortal flesh

Through the orifice of my heart

Where the veins of my soul begins

Deep within the depths of the locket

That evokes the brevity of my thoughts

And embarks on a journey of self-discovery

Through the memories of my ancestors

That burns within the locket of my heart

And consumes the essence of my soul

As I gaze through the height of the new moon

And embrace the sight of the new dawn

Until the frailty of my heart is exposed

Through the door of the locket

That shutters under the sound of my voice

As I whisper the words, "Lonesome No More"

Through the depths of my heart

That rages through the tempest of my soul

Until I am alone no more

People with broken hearts feel like they are entitled to do whatever they want in order to protect what was left within. Constantly, they operate as a victim internally. They feel as though someone owes them for their affliction. It is easy for a victim to hold on to pain. It is not easy to let it go. I believe that it is important to understand pain and not act upon it. It is not fun to be blind by ones own pain. What benefit is it to hold on to it? Both parties have experienced pain. The one who is going through it and the one who is inflicting it. The cycle of pain continues and the end result is misery. No one is happy. It is no different than when your body responds to physical pain. The body interprets what needs to be done in order to protect itself. The difference is that the body knows its own healing process sometimes leaving visible scars. Unfortunately, when it comes to emotional pain, it is buried deep within the mind of the individual. The invisible wounds are painful reminders of the trauma they had experienced. You have to decide whether you want to be ruled by the lie. It is your choice. There are many facets of events that can precipitate the person's pain. The one thing everyone of us has in common is that we all know what pain feels like. We sometimes forget that we are not alone. I understand there are emotional barriers that need to be addressed. Pain produces more pain until there is *"Beauty From Pain,"* Artist: by SuperChick.

This type of person cries out for help in more ways than one. When someone has reached rock bottom, with no one to turn too, he will do things to mask whatever pain he was feeling. This may help him in the short term, but eventually the pain catches up with him, sometimes taking on a different form. We all handle pain differently. My mom came up with a unique concept to describe this type of person; "HURT SCREAMS LOUD." People lash out in all directions, not realizing the pain they were masking. All they wanted was for the pain to go away never to return. People can be hard on themselves. God offers grace and mercy to anyone who wants to receive it. All the person needs to do is accept God's grace, but that can be difficult if the person is constantly beating up themselves. Many circumstances have lies compounded on top of each other. In most cases people don't even know what was the original lie. As I am writing this, I am reminded of the pain I was concealing for many years. People try their best to cope with whatever they are feeling.

Coping skills don't work for some people because those skills don't allow them to face the problem. I don't mean actual physical confrontation, but coming to a resolution internally about whatever issues faced or felt. It is important to identify the next step beyond your coping, and I don't mean adding another type of coping skill. What is the motivation behind your coping and how does one look past and accept or deny within ourselves the struggles of what we have endured in our lives? How can we use our pain to inspire others to promote change within ourselves and our society? This could be difficult depending on how deep the scars were. The allure and/or trap with coping is that one can give off the illusion of happiness behind a sad veil, because each locked door lies the brokenness of an empty vessel that was shun away by false dreams, expectations, and tragic events. There is also the fact that you are constantly feeding your coping mechanism until it doesn't work anymore instead of trying to find ways of dealing with the problem. What solutions have you found in your coping skills? What have you learned through the process of coping? There are three areas on which one could focus on in order to achieve healing. First, they need to look deep within themselves to find what's causing them pain. By connecting or reconnecting with the Creator this can be accomplished. Second, understand that no matter what the situation may look like, He will never leave them, nor forsake them. You are not alone. God has changed my viewpoint in life. All the previous things I thought about Him were lies. Third, cleaning the body of toxins that can affect the person's mood as well as health is an important step. Bodily toxins is not the only area in life you should focus on. Cleaning out your past of anything toxic should be a focus as well. It is necessary to mentally detoxify the way you think by removing and/or add things that will help you change. This could mean unhealthy relationships and activities that have not benefited you. It is important to listen to your heart and not be in self denial about something you know is wrong. I know this will be difficult. People tend to gravitate towards what familiar them. That is why change is not easy and doesn't happen overnight. There are good habits and bad ones. It is important to recognize ones own self worth and this would include our beliefs. Another area of difficulty for a majority of people is becoming effective listeners.

Listening is a lost art these days. How can anyone get anything done when you have two birds chattering at the same time? The lie is that everything we have to do and want to say is more important than what the other person has to say. Therefore we are distracted from listening completely. It is interesting when you have two or more opposing belief systems clashing against each other for dominance. The end result of not listening effectively can be misunderstandings or bad forms of communication. Even though someone may have a different opinion, it doesn't mean that they are living a lie. There are rules that govern society when it comes to certain subjects that basically boils down to do no harm. It is important to both parties to try and understand each other. What is the goal of the conversation, to win, or to lose, to hurt, or to understand? I came up with a concept that could help in this area, because being able to listen to what the person is saying without getting argumentative is vital, especially if you want to get to the root of the lie. I have said to my parent in many discussions that it is better to talk without getting upset, raising your voice, or making facial gestures. Proper communication is imperative; so how do we approach this? I call the concept EAR: **E**ngage-**A**ssess-**R**esolve. First, you engage the person in the conversation to see where they stand and to get to know their circumstances. Next, you assess the situation by evaluating the information. Lastly, you should resolve the issue or lie so that there is some type of agreeable outcome. The goal is not to win or lose in the conversation but to communicate and share ideas. Conflict resolution is important. The end result of some confrontation varies, but the rewards can be fulfilling. The only way this can be accomplished is by listening to the person which is the function of the ear.

Wherefore, my beloved brethren, let every man be swift to hear, slow to speak, slow to wrath (James 1:19 KJV).

There is a continuation to, "The Baby and The Gold

Piece." Ask yourself this, where did the gold piece come from? Did the piece of gold come from a lie or a truth? When it comes to things we have received in life, is it really to our benefit to have or to want based on our own views? The idea of wanting something and being willing enough to do whatever it takes to get it, even if that means crossing a few boundaries, doesn't hold truth. What type of riches are worth for the price of our souls? The price through which we sow you shall surely reap. How much is it really worth to sacrifice our time, energy, and being for something we may want to receive? Do we really understand the cost of that sacrifice? Do we comprehend the responsibility we have to ourselves or each other and embrace the truth? It is important to understand where someone's values take them because the individual knows their limitations regardless of the outcome. The consequence remains the same and that will be revealed in due time. Who or what defines your values?

The circumstances I have faced have become more revealing to me. I have been labeled a lie even though what I am saying is the truth. The truth has become a blur in my world and I would not wish this world on my worst enemy. There are too many problems or lies going on everyday that are considered cloak and dagger. Finding out the truth has become more important to me. I can't help but wonder what happened to truth these days? The term action speaks louder than words holds more meaning for me.

My little children let us not love in word, neither in tongue but in deed and in truth (1 John 3:18 KJV).

People should look in the mirror to realize if they truly like what they see. Take a long look. What do you see in yourself? What is the first thought that comes in your belief system? How does it affect you when you see your reflection? When I look in the mirror I see possibilities and hope. I am a smart individual with plenty of life ahead of me and I will not let anything deter me from what I believe to be true. Of course, this is all looking at the surface, but we all have to start from somewhere.

Mini Reflection

I look out through the window

Through the glass

The first thing I see is me

Me?

Not you

The thought of seeing a world beyond the reflection becomes a distraction

I raise one arm and you copy

Who are you?

I'm me

No, I'm you

Stop it!

The person mocks me

A splash of reality comes to me

Walk away

For now we see through a glass darkly; but then face to face: now I know in part; but then shall I know even as also I am known (1 Corinthian 13:12 KJV).

Unfortunately, when a person is living a lie, he creates

ripples that spread in all directions. There is a force, or rock, that causes ripples in peoples' lives. This influence causes other ripples to form. The stones are a representation of a truth or lie being tossed into the sea of life. These stones symbolize good or bad choices. Eventually, the person will have so many rocks or lies gathered in one place until what they consider to be a mole hill can turn into a mountain. This height in elevation represents consequences. As one stares at what seems to be a impossible situation, he begins to contemplate whether those past decisions were really worth it. We are living in a world with good and bad consequences. The effects of ones choices in life varies, but it is essential to understand the consequences of our actions even if the outcome was amusing.

You know, I have been serious with this subject, but there are a few cases where lies can be comical. For example, here I am trying to type this manuscript when all of sudden a button on my keyboard stops working and my internet crashes. I frantically tried everything to get the colon button to work; not only that. My document starts doing some weird things with the control button. I started thinking the worst, and proceeded to scan the system for any potential viruses that maybe trying to steal my work. All I can say is that it took a village to solve the problem. In the end I realized that I was pressing the wrong button. I was hitting the control key instead of the shift key. We were all over the place trying to figure out why this function was not working. Let's just say, "that the truth will set you free." It is good to laugh at ones self. You'll find that laughter can be great medicine. I find that humor shared with others can be healthy and necessary. Who doesn't like a good laugh? This lie was due to me being human and thinking that just because bad things were happening in that moment doesn't mean that it is truth. I am not perfect and neither are you because everyone make mistakes. We learn more from our failures than our successes.

A merry heart doeth good like a medicine: but a broken spirit drieth the bones (Proverb 17:22 KJV).

Countenance Of My Heart

A wounded mom

A lost son

Be taken and beaten

Being moved with tears

Be weave with grief

Separated by what was left of me

Wandering through the thicken of things

Reaching towards Thee

For answers of heaven's pleaded

What to say but "Oh why me?"

Moving past the deepen sea

Being swept away by broken leaves

Each step bringing me closer to my destiny

The healing of a broken soul

When shall this be?

Oh take this away from me

Prickly thorns and trouble sores

Searching for the newness of me

Thou who believes in Thee

To carry us through life's troubled plead

Overwhelmed by joyful tithes

Keep this in mind

He has done it all

For you and me

The love so deep

Surrender to Thee

Oh what must I do to weep

My Savior where is He?

The one who never leaves me

In this mortal shell of dust

He dwell within each of us

Showing leniency

Healing me

I have a message I want to share with you, but I don't know how you will receive it. I can only pray that it will touch you. Look at the face of your child and see their expression. The face is the window that pierces into the unknown and wonders about the things of this world we live in. Don't silence it. Let it experience peace knowing that you care. It is my desire that the reader looks at the face of their child and wonders what they are feeling about them. This is a letter hoping to obtain that very thing.

A *Child's Message*

"You don't care about your children. You don't care about our feelings, you don't care about what we have gone through. If you had you would acknowledge your part in it and

at least apologized, but you haven't. To care is to live and I want to live. I didn't care enough. I thought about what you said constantly. It was something that brought me to this breaking point. My body was screaming at me. It has experienced such pain. I feel like it has every right to be angry with me."

"The sleepless nights. Do you know what it feels like to be taken from your mother at the age of three not knowing why and wondering if you had done anything wrong to cause it? Or forbidden to go to her or my sister when I saw them in public. Or to be constantly screamed at for the smallest thing and then being called stupid to the point that you started to believe it. Or to be starving at school because you were too afraid to ask for money for lunch. Or to be bullied or made fun of the majority of the days at school. Or being so distraught every single day that you didn't care about your hygiene when you went to the bathroom. Or to want desperately your father love, but could not figure out how to get it. This is nowhere what I have gone through because of that initial act."

"Now to be diagnosis with schizophrenia and possible

tourettes. Even that is not my fault. None of this has been my fault. I try not to have the mindset of why me, but it is just not fair. They say that it comes from trauma or lost at an early age. They say that it comes from years of buildup. Where is your place in this? Are you free from any accountability? No. Whether you acknowledge it or not does not change the truth. I have had some good things happen in spite of this but everyday its hard."

"For years I had no voice, whether it be from fear of retribution, or because it was just not being heard. I am not going to stuff my feelings any longer. I may not receive a responds back, but at least, I will get to say what I finally feel. My life is definitely at a crossroad and I am afraid which way it is going. Still so much uncertainty."

"Someday you will realize what special children you have. All smart, all good looking, all compassionate. Each with their own unique requirements for love. With the Lord's help I have been working on forgiving you and I actually do love you. That has not been easy for me because even though I have not lived with you for years the effects of living with you

lingers. That is what I am trying to get past. There are people here trying to help but it is you that needs to know these things."

"I pray this will make an impact on you. I have no control over what you do from here on out. I cannot let that concern me. I need to continue to focus on my health. If I have to do so without you, so be it."

"As your child all I ever wanted to here from you was a sincere apology. Maybe if I had turned left instead of right I probably wouldn't have ended up in this situation. Someday you will take that unwanted step of getting closer to your children. Until then you should know that I'm going to be moving on with my life. I hope you don't make the same mistakes with your new family as you did with your old one. I hope you show them the love and respect they are so rightfully due."

"It is my prayer that one day when someone is reading this book that they may find peace knowing that they aren't alone in their pain. The kind of peace not bestowed upon from man, but given from the one who can bare their burdens."

"May the Lord bless you and keep you..."

— *Jonathan*

The Nature of Unbelief

I didn't believe because I equated my heavenly Father to my earthly one. How many times must I deny myself the truth? I fell short of the mark. The very nature of unbelief is endowed by the essence of chaos and confusion. The chaos within my heart that was formed from my very own unbelief. The human heart is exceedingly wicked and tries its best to exalt itself over the living God. The lessons of life continues and the ignorance of man knows no bounds. What do I believe...what do I truly believe in my heart? Ask yourself this question why is it so hard to believe in God, because He is the representation of love, hope, joy, redemption, and revelation. God is the same as He was yesterday, today, and tomorrow so how can one individual not believe on such things if they did not see this for themselves? There is no stability in unbelief.

What I have gleamed from the parable, "The Sower of The Seeds" is that it sounds like to me different forms of unbelief. I believe that the sower of the seeds is Jesus Christ or the believer and that the seeds represent the Word of God. I also believe that the soil represent the heart through which the seeds can germinate. The chronicles of the living where your faith can either be eaten up, choked out, scorched, or grow in good soil. The constructs within the parable can represent different forms of circumstances that the believer experiences throughout their life that challenges their faith. The seeds that are eaten along the path by the bird represent Satan devouring the word from the believer. The seeds that fall on the stony ground are not rooted or grounded in there faith, so when the sun shines on them the pressures of life reveals who they really are until they are scorched. These seeds represent the Word being received by the person hearing from it that affects the individual's internal or external circumstances within the believer's life. The thorns within the parable could represent the Word being choked by the different forms of illegitimate beliefs, or actions that doesn't benefit the believer's growth. This is all depended on you and what you choose to accept or reject in your life in regards to God's words.

The opposite of unbelief is to have faith, which is believing in God and His words. How much is it really worth to have a faith the size of a musters seed? It can mean so much more to those of us who have become believers. Please try to understand that faith is the substance of things hope for in the evidence of things not seen. I have been struggling throughout my entire life to have some level of faith in God. It is my hope that everything will workout for me in the end. It is better to have a faith that grows then to have no faith at all. How do you know when your seed has fallen on good soil? A soil that allows your faith to grow and not wither, or be choked up by the thorns and the thistles of this world – a seed that can move mountains. I believe that this growth can only occur when you have finally realize who you are in Christ and that this transformative power of your faith begins to mature. It is not enough for you to say what you believe. You must find yourself somewhere inside of Him. The person who He created you to be through His body. This is what I like to call, "Spiritual Maturation." The process through which a person reaches spiritual maturity. How do we know when you have reached a level of maturity? The question you should be asking yourself is where do you stand with your faith? What areas in your life do you still need to improve when it comes to your unbelief? We should be conscientious in our growth as we walk towards the straight and narrow gate with God in our lives. The process of seeding starts the moment we look deep within ourselves. As the little seed begins to grow into a state of consciousness, the embryonic state of the seed must die in order for the plant to thrive. I believe that this rich fertile soil represents the experiences we have learned throughout our lives that the Lord uses to help us grow in our faith. As the seed gets rooted through the dust of the Earth, the plant begins to grow through the dirt of life until it has blossomed into the peak of freshness. As we begin to mature, the fruit of our labor begins to permeate throughout our thoughts until every little grain of seedling begins to grow within ourselves and each other. We are spiritual like beings living in a natural existence, while in a state of decay; the natural cycle of life. For there is a time and place for everything: a time to give birth, a time of rebirth, and a time of death in the eyes of humanity. As humans we go through these cycles of life and death with every phase of incubation rejuvenating us in the thoughts and minds of the believer giving birth to a new creation. For we are creatures of cycles with seasons of fresh renewal until we have reached the final stage of our existence and gaze through the eyes of the Eternal. As mere mortal we must appreciate the nuances of this gift. The gift of breathing in and out through these shallow slow breaths that surpasses all understanding beyond the borders of this physical body. For this mortal shell of dust maybe in a state of atrophy, but the Spirit of God lives on within each of us. The Spirit of God whispers, guides, and comforts us. The Spirit of God moves us down the path towards the truth. It is the still quiet small voice that sows the seeds within our hearts. I would like the Spirit of Truth to encapsulate my soul and heal my broken heart from my very own unbelief. The Lord is transforming me with every little grain of muster seed – a transition from death to life. As for my unbelief...well; I still have some growing to do in my own belief system.

The unbelief heart wonders around in the wilderness searching for what was lost from without and within only to find nothing more then heartache. Where is the promise land in my heart? Where is this land that flows with milk and honey? I want my heart to be restored to its former glory. I know that is no longer possible because that would mean resurrecting the old me. If the Lord is searching out my heart, why not me? I have changed since my break. It is hard to imagine that my unbelief would lead me down a path towards redemption. I have to let go of my unbelief and the lie that was produced from it. How do I fully let go and accept that my break did happen to me? How can I believe that everything is going to be alright? I had lost the will to believe. Where is my faith? I am so tired...

I have struggled for a very longtime trying to find the answers to these questions that would give me some level of peace. I didn't believe, nor did I care anymore. I must accept that fact. It is hard to accept reality, but I think it is even worst in my opinion to be living in a fantasy. A place where things are not real, and the struggles of creating memories within oneself becomes empty.

I did not realize my ignorance, nor did I presumed the consequences of my actions caused by my own unbelief. How arrogant was I to think that there was no God and that I could do it all by myself. The past...the present...the future...it all means absolutely nothing to Him, but at the same time it means everything to us; because our lives are finite. The time we have on this planet maybe small, but compare to eternity this is nothing. The little moments we do have as specks of dust holds a significant piece to a very important puzzle. We are mortal beings serving a infinite God who is eternal. My life would have been all for naught if it weren't for the fact that He was involved in it.

In whom the god of this world hath blinded the minds

of them which believe not, lest the light of the glorious gospel of Christ, who is the image of God, should shine unto them (2 Corinthian 4:4 KJV).

I was blinded by the circumstances in my life until my eyes were open to something far worst then what I had experienced. My mind became vulnerable to the events surrounding my break. I saw and experienced things that would send shivers down your spine. Why didn't I believe? Why did this happen to me? Someone please tell me...why!?

The pain within my heart was unbearable and the source of my unbelief. Deep down I was angry with God for my troubles and had felt like He had forsaken me. Why should I believe in Him, or anyone else for that matter? My feelings were clouded and I felt like He owed me for the pains I had received in my life. My heart was filled with so much vengeance and grief. I had lost hope...

I ran away from God and tried my best to run away from myself. I am tired of running, it can be exhausting work. It is hard to believe, but that is the very nature of unbelief. I believed on not believing on Him and relied on my own judgments. It was a lie. How selfish and foolish was I to think that I could circumvent the will of the living God. I deceived myself by believing this lie. What sense could I have drawn upon in my own life? I felt lost and betrayed by Him and those closest to me. It is hard to fathom the very nature of this journey, and the struggles that comes along with it. It is hard to imagine that there is life beyond this world. Should I believe, or not believe in this other world? A world filled with no pain or sorrow. I believe...I believe...I be...

I have experienced everything from pains on my body to verbal tics. Is it real? I can feel it from the depths of my soul. It is real to me. I am Christian and a believer. As I cry out to the heavens, "I Believe!"

Take heed, brethren, lest there be in any of you an evil heart of unbelief, in departing from the living God (Hebrews 3:12 KJV).

Tapestry

Through loneliness comes thought

Through patience comes results

Through mercy and strife

Through death there is life

Through sickness and health

Through blindness and sight

Through challenges of this life

Through what perceives to be the end

Through what is hard to comprehend

Through daily chores and activities

Through what this journey means to me

Through rain, storm, and sleet

Through constant battles and evermore peace

Through treacherous waters and raging seas

Through life's ever growing destiny

Through faith and unbelief

Through truth that lies beneath

Through knowing The Prince of Peace

Through all eternity

LIES IN MANY FORMS

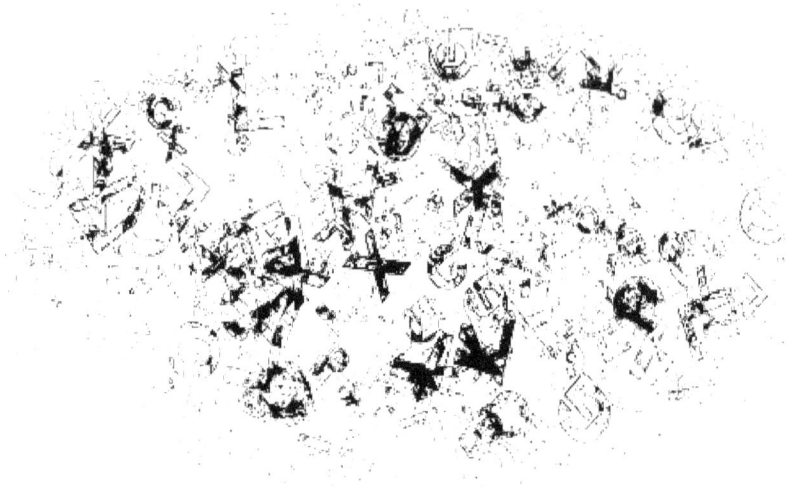

We all know that it is not good to tell lies, but what about lying to yourself? Lying to yourself about something can be devastating. Facing and accepting the truth about yourself can be the hardest thing anyone can do. It is important to know who you are and to not accept certain things into your belief system. I can relate in some ways, but people need to understand and realize that what they are doing will not benefit them. I know this will require some courage, and it maybe painful, but once you have faced it. You will have a sense of relief about whatever lie you were not willing to accept. Hiding the truth about yourself will only put more pressure on you as an individual until something has to give.

What becomes more important to us will determine how we respond. I am trying to understand my feelings. I am hurt. I am sad and confused. I don't know whats going to happen next in my life.

I feel like I am being tossed to and fro by the northern seas of life with ever wind of doctrine sweeping beneath my feet crushing my solid foundation. I am not a innocent bystander when it comes to truth and lies. Life has many contradictions even when it comes to how we view ourselves. I want to be whole again, but I don't know how to deal with the trauma of my past. We all want to have more things out of life, but we don't want to bear the burden of receiving more from it, and maybe we are too afraid to face what we cannot understand; like me having a mental break. I have struggled with accepting the truth surrounding those events. The only statement that I can come up with is that you cannot have your cake and eat it too. A person must take some level of ownership when it comes to dealing with things in their life, but also be willing enough to forgive one self and let go of the pain. We are all conflicting creatures with so many things working against us. I am a walking contradiction like everyone else. There are so many conflicting things happening within me, and so many questions as well. What can I do to rise above this victim mentality and establish a sense of wholeness? How can one get to the point of forgiving their past and seize the essence of what lies before them? How can we push beyond the boundaries of ourselves to move pass our circumstances when it comes to people? We all have fallen short in many aspects of our lives. I too, have told my fair share of lies in my lifetime to myself and others. I'm in no position to cast the first stone, nor preach about things without looking at myself first, but I am so tired of being disrespected, used, abused, and manipulated by people. I am a broken person trying to reach broken people whose inner world has been shrouded in darkness. We can't run away from ourselves, nor should we even try; believe me it doesn't end well. But how can we fight this inner demon caused by the circumstances within our lives?

How can anyone find themselves under these conditions?

When it comes to finding yourself and your place in the world. You shouldn't put a label on yourself and expect to live to that expectation. People tend to put labels on others that may not be true about that person. People need to be careful and not make false assumptions about other individuals. The only label I care about is what the Lord has given me. When people do that they limit the picture of that individual. Allow the person to tell their story the way it is suppose to be told. It is important to understand ones own expectations and the motivation behind it. There needs to be a balance between the two because each day I'm learning something new about myself. All I can say to you is live...live every moment...never take it for granted. Be real. It takes time and effort to discover what lie you have been believing.

There are some people who believe a lie out of laziness, or because someone has a title to their name. I find this odd only because God has given us the mental capacity to think for ourselves. Here is another analogy the Father has given me. You are walking in the park with some people and you come across a talking statue that looks like a person. The statue tries to get your attention with information you should hear. The people stop to listen to what the sculpture has to say. All of a sudden, animals gather around the statue. A dog...a cat....some birds, and they began to chatter. The people listen to the structure for a while and then walk away. The animals stay to listen, not realizing what the statue is saying to them whether it is to their benefit or not. Who are the animals and who are the people? People have the ability to have a mind of their own, but don't exercise it on a regular basis. They listen to any type of information without investigating the problem for themselves, or questioning what is being told to them is truth. Animals have very small brains, but we don't. I am not trying to sound insulting. I am just trying to make a point.

The simple believeth every word: but the prudent man looketh well to his going (Proverb 14:15 KJV).

For the leaders of this people cause them to err; and they that are led of them are destroyed (Isaiah 9:16 KJV).

I was always told by some people that I have a mouth, but I have not accepted this truth, and I am not going to start now. I draw the line before cursing, but sometimes my mouth has slipped a few words that would either leave people laughing on the floor, or leave a few blank faces with cricket sounds going on in the background. My first truth was when I was little, and I said this to my grand-father, "Gran-pa you have no hair." He responded and said, "You live long enough you won't either." Don't worry, I have changed for the better since I was little. I have learned that it is better to say nothing, than to say anything at all.

Some people don't want to hear the truth from you no matter how nice you say it only because it is too painful. I can understand individuals who want to help the person who is hurting in some form or fashion, but they have to realize what lie they have been believing on there own. You can guide them to the truth, but the direct approach doesn't always work in order for them to obtain, "*Victory,*" Artist: by Yolanda Adams.

I can't help but wonder, once the person has achieved

victory what's next? Once again the person needs to look deep within themselves. Ask the Father what is it that the person can do to help others realize that they are not alone. What talents can you utilize in order to help others? I can say this, that it depends on the person's experiences and knowledge. When dealing with people it is better to release all negative emotions. Once this has been accomplished, you can think more clearly. This could lead to other possibilities that you probably would not have thought of if the circumstances were different.

There is one body, and one Spirit, even as ye are called in one hope of your calling (Ephesian 4:4 KJV).

Accepting the truth sometimes only requires the person to just say, "*Yes,*" Artist: Shekinah Glory Ministry.

I find it rewarding to see the person come to the truth about whatever lie he was believing, especially if that lie was painful. God does not want to see his children in pain for whatever reason. He wants us to love one another, and advance His kingdom by bringing others to the same truth.

This is my commandment. That ye love one another, as I have loved you (John 15:12 KJV).

How do you navigate in this world among deceivers, and the deceived? I believe that it is important to be aware of both parties by observing your surroundings and be true to one self. It is easy to get caught into something that you don't know or understand. The key lies in knowing what your boundaries are and being educated with the subject. Surprisingly, deceivers many times are also deceived. They may feel smarter or justified to do whatever they want whether it hurts others or not. The best advice I can give when dealing with someone who play games with others is to avoid the individual. People who play with your emotions, mix lie and truth together. This causes the individual to not have an idea on the player's true intentions. You run the risk of receiving from both the lie and the truth. Situations where both lie and truth are present can be very harmful, especially if the person puts his trust in the individual. Playing games with people's emotions are obviously wrong, but there are ways to deal with the situation if you know where to look. I believe the person should first think about why he has put his trust in this individual in the first place. They should then try their best to focus on the connectors to the lie, because you already know what the truth is about the person who hurt you.

For example, "I thought the person cared about me," and that would be a normal response.

The individual needs to be able to heal from the experience by identifying all lies, so that the truth is more clear. Everyone grieves at their own pace, and talking to someone can help, as long as they don't solely focus on the event, or get the person riled-up. Fortunately, time heals all wounds. The road to recovery maybe difficult, but once the person has achieved some type of resolution, moving past the event becomes easier. The goal is not to focus on the act, but to place emphasis on what led the individual to believe the lie in the first place, which would minimize it happening again. The truth is that the person who caused you pain has more issues to deal with than you do.

Earlier I spoke about how surprisingly many deceivers

are deceived. People need to step back from their circumstances and get a different perspective. I want individuals to be able to analyze his or her own actions, and focus on figuring out their thought patterns when it comes to certain situations. Understanding where the lie originated will help formulate different ways of coming up with solutions to a problem. The telling of truth and lies is as old as the dirt beneath our feet.

I just want to make something clear for people that I am not condoning the act of not telling the truth or that it is okay to tell a lie. I want people to think about what lies or truth that they have been believing within themselves. There is a difference between introspecting the truth and/or lies within our lives that people have been believing on a regular bases and situational type moral dilemmas where you need to decide whether to tell the truth or a lie. There is a line of demarcation between the distinction of situational and introspection. The difference between the two lies in the fact that situational start from the outside in, while introspection starts from the inside out. However, this doesn't mean that they do not coincide with each other, because depending on the situation the results of the circumstances can cause individuals to think about the decisions that they have made and react accordingly.

What is the difference between believing a lie and living one? The difference is a simple matter of process. You first have to believe a lie. The belief of that lie has to be strong enough where it influences your decisions. How do you know when someone is living a lie? The decisions the person makes will often answer this question and the consequences can be life changing. Unfortunately, there are some people who are not willing to accept their circumstances until something happens. The events involved with the person usually will cause a response, but this type of reaction is only temporary. The person has reacted to the situation and has not admitted that they need to change. If people want to change, they have to come to that determination themselves. Change does not come easy for most individuals, especially if they were raised to think a certain way. There is always a chance for anyone to receive healing. The desire to want a new direction in one's life can be powerful enough to give people a drive that will enable them to overcome any challenges. The difficulties of today are that people are constantly moving in one way or another. Individuals need to slow down and take a look around them. The actions of many can be perceived as being reckless or irresponsible, but I see it as a cry for help. I believe that when someone is living a lie they are living contrary to what God wants them to be. No one is living in complete truth including me. We all have areas in our lives where we need to change our belief system. Please understand this is not about living a perfect life where you don't experience any type hardship. This is about what you believe shapes your reality. I know this is difficult to hear, but how can you grow if you don't experience some pruning in your life. I don't like to get hurt either, but I look at this way things could be worst. Where does the lie begin and the truth end? No matter what you say, or what you do it is not going to change the truth.

A State of Being

I look at the world and see things moving

People walking

Talking

Everything but understanding

I stare and wonder

What does my world look like

Everyone is framed, and put together

They have everything you can imagine

Blue Skies, and sunshine

Rocky Trails, and moonlight tails

I look and see that I am not framed

As I search for my foundation

People stare

I begin to wonder what are they looking at

As I walk I see that each frame is different

Heavy...Light

Dumb...Smart

Each with its own characteristics

I walk around and come across a shop

People walking in and out

Their frames have improved

Shiny and expensive

I walk into the shop only to be kicked out

I continue...

I want a frame

Where is my frame?

Did someone take it?

Did I loose it?

Head Down

As I walk I see myself fading away

I come across an abandoned frame

Cracked...Used...Abused

I put it on

After walking with no picture

The story becomes clear

I am BRUISED

By mercy and truth iniquity is purged: and by the fear of the Lord men depart from evil (Proverb 16:6 KJV).

The lies people create can affect everyday life, and this would include sale outs, or individuals who have sacrificed themselves in order to get ahead. Regardless, if anyone gets hurt, these type of individuals have lost something more and believe that they will benefit in the end. Unfortunately, the connections the person has made with people are not real. This type of lie can work both ways because the individual is living a lie, and thus everything about his life is a fantasy. WAKE UP! I don't want to get preachy. Regrettably, these people only care about themselves and they may not realize it, but they are being used too. In my opinion, the time for change is now and doing so will allow them to make genuine connections with people. Sadly enough, these types of individuals are in all areas of our society; truth is truth. For how much do you have to sell yourself in order to make it in this world? In regards to this subject, it is best to watch out for the mole that is on your lawn. What does that mean? You figure it out.

Which have forsaken the right way, and are gone astray, following the way of Balaam the son of Bosor, who loved the wages of unrightousness (2 Peter 2:15 KJV).

I have struggled for a long time trying to put the pieces back together. I want to be happy, but I don't know what that means anymore. In the mist of my experiences, I believe that it will eventually work out. It is going to take time. I have been looking at myself and I didn't like what I saw. I had lost my identity to the pains of the past. People are not always going to be ready to look deep within themselves. The person I was is not who I want to be. There is life somewhere inside of me. A place where truth resides and the lies of many forms are expelled.

THE QUIET PLACE

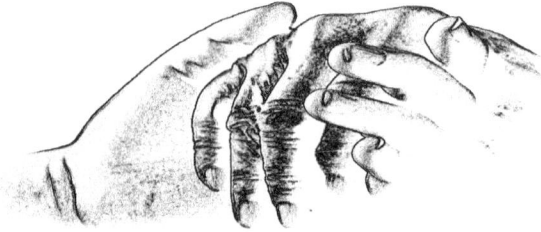

I have talked about lies, but what about truth? There is a place where truth dwells and has nothing but peace. The quiet place that will reveal so much in your life. You are calm and clear about who you are if you understand the truth within. There is only you and the Father who is calling you with only a whisper of his soft but mighty voice. I know you have been waiting for a long time. It's time to be free from all forms of lies and dwell in truth. I have to be honest, I do not know what you maybe going through and our situations will be different, but one thing is constant and that is truth. The Lord wants you to understand His truth, so you may enter into a place of stability with a firm foundation. I have been operating out of pain for far too long and need to return to the quiet place.

I am trying to understand truth myself, but that is why I'm doing my best to understand me before I was introduced to lies. The quiet place in your heart beats and the pain you feel will not last long. Allow God to show you what truth really means in the quiet place. The peace He will bring in your life will offer so much joy, even during times of great distress. The quiet place is a place of complete silence. It is not a physical place. It is where God has positioned you to hear Him more clearly and know His truth. The quiet place is where someone's beliefs rest with Him. Ask God to reveal Himself to you. I had moments in the quiet place where things became clear after having so many distractions in my life. All I wanted was for my life to be smooth, but I didn't know how or what to do. I asked the Lord to, "*Reveal Your Glory*," Artist: Vicki Yohe.

The Quiet Place

There is a quiet place where He dwells

Called

The Great I Am

Who ask for naught

An invitation...A declaration

He who is Holy

The quiet place

Where you see nothing but Him and His glory

His gentle demeanor calm and wonderful

Lend to you His child

As we look towards the quiet place

The wonder of Him begins to set in until we hear, "Be Not Afraid"

I Am...in the quiet place

The quiet place is with Jesus Christ as our Lord and Savior. He quiets our hearts, he quiets our mind. This is the only place where healing can form. It is only in His presence that truth can be revealed. My position was compromised for a long time. There is a place of truth that people search for, but do not know how to obtain it. I am trying to understand the quiet place, but that will take time. I am alright with it. The journey I am on will open up new doors with God in the forefront. I will have my opportunity to understand the quiet place. The pains of the past are becoming more distance. The

Lord wants to reveal Himself to you. Allow God to bear the burdens you have kept and let go of the pain. This new chapter called, "The Quiet Place" is a new position that the Lord is placing within me. I may never fully understand the quiet place, but I will try. I don't even know how to describe it. All I know is this place...

People spend their entire lives trying to define what makes them happy - have a purpose. The only person I can speak for is me. What is happening to me is unique. I am constantly changing and understanding. I have more respect for myself than in times past. I looked back and wondered why would I disrespect myself? When I enter into the quiet place every problem becomes trivial. I am at peace and the truth becomes more appealing to me. I want God to show me more and help me with my growth. I ask you to consider your position and look around you. What makes you happy? What do you think will make Him happy? Are you at peace with yourself? What motivates your choices in life? I cannot answer these questions for you. I can't define you as a person, nor can I tell you what is right. Ask the Father to show you because He is nothing but truth. The struggles we have endured in our lives can also provide a greater meaning for ourselves and someone else. The desire we all share is to try and find that meaning to our very own existence. It is my hope that the journey I am on is leading me down a path towards the truth.

I am currently trying to understand truth. I may have said the meaning of the word truth, but that doesn't mean I understand it completely. People can define truth, but to understand it that requires direction from God. I don't have all the answers to this subject. All I can do is to continue moving forward and allow the Lord to show me what I need to know. I can't force the answers, but I have faith and hope that He will reveal the many treasures within me in the quiet place.

And my people shall dwell in a peaceable habitation, and in sure dwellings, and in quiet resting places; (Isaiah 32:18 KJV).

The Power of Self

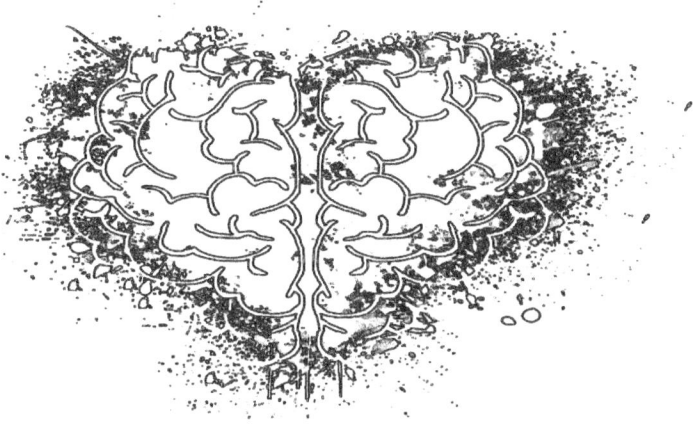

I have questioned the power of self many times in my life, and have given myself to the lies of this world. The pressure to remain authentic can be overwhelming, especially when you are on a journey of self-discovery. The circumstances surrounding my mental break, the lost of my identity, and the shattered essences of self. Why must I go through the cycles of grief? How can I understand what will make me happy when I am afraid to show my own shadow? How am I suppose to showcase my own humanity? What is wrong with me for being different? What is wrong with me for being special? What is wrong with me? The death of self came at an early age.

The power of self-motivation holds a key to understanding the power of self. What does it all mean for you when I use this word called, "Self?" What sense of self am I referring too? I am talking about, "You." How do you feel about yourself? There are some days I feel happy and other days I feel sad. The experience of what we receive from life constantly changes and influences us on many different levels. This would include, but not limited too our: physical, subconscious, environmental, sociological, spiritual, and economic beliefs. What is self and how does one obtain a level of understanding of oneself? The dynamics of self-awareness is endowed by the essence of ones own consciousness and being cognitive enough to the many facets within those perceptions. The characteristics of these ideals shape and mold us through a series of constructs that can elevate, humble, create, or destroy us in someway. We are creature of creation and destruction made by the Creator to uphold the many principles that was laid down before the foundation of the world. We should always be aware that we carry within us the power to shape reality and bend it to our will. People seem to be more interested in having a dialogue with each other, but no one seems to be interested in having a dialogue with oneself. We are constantly being bombarded with conflicting notions about who or what we are in terms of self. We are like a sophisticated form of a Chameleon who camouflages and blends in with our surroundings in order to conform to our circumstances, beliefs, and environment. Human-beings are a living contradiction in terms of the quality of our nature. We tend to gravitate more easily to our negative side rather than our positive ones. Also, we tend to switch our various nature from negative to positive and visa versa depending on our circumstances. The concept of self is the quality of what makes us human. The idea of individuality allows the dynamics to change even further. We all have unique fingerprints with different views and belief systems; like a snowflake falling from the sky. These commonality traits can also allow us to embrace our own personal identity. Please allow yourself time to find the answers. Ask questions about yourself. Who are you and what do you like, or don't like about yourself? What have you accepted or denied within yourself? You need to try and understand how important you are to yourself and the world. You need to make a decision and choose to speak, think, and act when it comes to your life. We can be our greatest cheerleader or our worst critic and are constantly at war with ourselves. I ask you these series of questions so you can think about how you view yourself. I don't have all the answers to these questions. Your views may not be the same as my views and visa versa. But it is important to understand the value of what makes us so unique. This is why we must be careful about what we allow to influence our minds. The influence of our beliefs start with the power of one.

You can't be so open minded that you allow anything and everything to penetrate the essence of who you are in terms of self. But you can't be so close minded either that you don't even try and understand the other person's point of view. There is a balance between open and close mindedness. It is not easy to find the straight and narrow gate of our lives - a place of clarity and peace. As human-beings we need to try our best to weigh in our decisions that should have a positive impact on other people. How much should a person endure in this world that's filled with so much controversy and contradictions? There is always two sides to every coin and each side can represent a truth or a lie about yourself and the world.

Why does transformation starts off in the dark and why is it so hard to step into the light? Where the essence of our secrets have been shun away by the shame of life, and the struggles of remaining authentic becomes a challenge. The beauty behind the meaning of darkness is that one can appreciate the nuances of being in the light. We are all being shaped by the darkness within our hearts by a master craftsmen. Please allow the light and darkness within your heart to shape you into something genuine. The exploration within ourselves starts the moment we begin to challenge our own minds. The process of stepping into the light from the essence of darkness is always painful, because each step reveals something new, or old about ourselves that we had rejected and/or accepted a longtime ago. The concept of being able to embrace both the light and the dark sides of ourselves allows us to appreciate the meaning behind both of their existence. They are both a part of us and rejecting one over the other, while embracing only half of who we are as individuals, will only lead us down a path towards self-destruction. We cannot embrace so much of the darkness and ignore the light because that would lead us down a path towards pain. But we also shouldn't embrace so much of the light either and ignore the darkness because that will lead us down a path towards a false sense of reality. The concept is no different when it comes to accepting the reality of individual's situations and/or circumstances. I have struggled with finding the balance between the two when it comes to my emotions and medical condition.

I have struggled with accepting myself and have immersed my essence in total darkness in order to protect myself from the world. These empty spaces in my heart must be filled, right!? I have prayed that this heart of mine will be unbroken and beat once again. Why must I carry this heavy burden alone? I feel so incomplete as my heartaches for Thee. I have a heart filled with so much hatred. How can one forgive one self and others? What is hope and where can I find it? Is it nothing more than a fantasy? Is it even real? It sometime feels like the pain is all I have left and that I am sleep walking. These feelings sometimes don't even feel real to me. I am so weak and such a coward. I sometimes feel like giving up. There has been so many voices within me that I have been fighting against for a very longtime. I want to be happy, but I don't know what I want anymore out of this life. I have been concealing myself for a very longtime. It is like hiding the core of my being on a blank canvas for no one to see or experience. Don't be afraid to showcase your emotions and colors. Use your imagination to fill in the blanks for yourself and see what cannot be seen underneath the blank canvas. For there are colors all around us that penetrates and binds us altogether. For these are the moments that captivates our curiosity of the world we live in through the eyes of a child – filled with such deep forms of emotional expressions and incubation. Don't be afraid to showcase your humanity. Show all your emotions and colors. There are colors inside of us filled with such vitality and life that is not so skin deep. For in order to see what cannot be seen one must peer into the windows of the unknown and seize what is unattainable – one must peer into the nuances of creation with humble grace and humility. Show all your splendor. For we are all children of the universe who are fearfully and wonderfully made with unique lives and perspectives. We are born as a child and we shall die as a child. I know this may have sounded a bit morbid in the beginning, but I have struggled with addressing my own needs.

The word, "Need" is such a powerful statement that often times goes unanswered. How often have we addressed the need of self? There is a difference between addressing what we want rather than what we need. I want to communicate my feelings effectively with people. I need to established a long lasting relationship and not be fearful to make those connections happen. I came up with a formula that should shed some light on this subject using myself as a Guinea-pig. The source of our needs lies in our own internal perceptions, and these perceptions can switch from our internal or external behaviors. First, write your name on the top of a sheet of paper and then circle it. Next, draw an arrow downward from your name. Then write the word, "Needs," and circle it. Second, think of your top three external needs and then write them down next to the word, "Needs." Lastly, I need for you to think about how these needs are affecting you internally. How is your internal needs based off of your external behavior and visa versa? These external and internal needs can be interchangeable and can play duo roles as well, so there is no right or wrong answer to this exercise. Why do you need them and how will they address your internal needs? The goal of this exercise is to look within ourselves to see what we truly need. Please understand, the needs of the individual will be different. My needs may not be the same as another person. So what is it that you need? I need emotional stability base off of my top three environmental needs. They include, but not limited to: social interactions or friends, being able to handle conflict, and a stable environment. This requires some emotional awareness, and being comfortable enough to tread in ones own mind. What is my emotional IQ and how does it affect the power of self? The journey to restore ones self starts the moment you wake up. The current dynamics of the next generation is based off of our own social and economic dispositions.

The difficulties of today's young people lies in the power of self; self-acceptance or self-rejection. You can't control what people think about you, but you can control what you think about yourself. The concept between the two lies in the power of the majority rather than the minority. This does not have to be true about you as a individual. These influences can cast a shadow on a person's perception of life, especially if they have low self-esteem. We shouldn't fall into the trap of self-pity or doubt about who we are in terms of self. The strength to maintain one self is an uphill battle. It requires self-discipline, strong conviction and the fortitude to not waiver in the face of such obstacles. The blind shall only see when they are able to embrace the power of self. It is important to know who you are and to maintain that sense of truth with a strong foundation. I can understand when one is overwhelmed by the pressures of life. The feeling of being casts into the deepest sea without knowing who you are, or how to navigate; it can be scary. Nevertheless, it is the extremely important to understand and not to hide yourself from the world. You are free...the bonds have been broken. The yoke has been torn asunder. So what are you waiting for? The seasons of life has fallen fresh anew for those who are fearless and are willing to accept the power of self.

Temperaments of a Blank Canvas

Deep in the world of poly-chromatic,

is a realm of pure substance

Filled with so many hues and saturation

That runs deep within my brush strokes

and goes beyond the void

Filled with such vitality and life,

while drawing on a White canvas

Using nothing but oils and pastels

My temperament is revealed

While fighting the urge to give up –

The urge to reveal myself

My emotions are filled with so many colors

These are the temperaments of a blank canvas

That evokes the essence of my spirit

and has kindled the elements of nature

Enticed by the allure of frankincense and myrrh

Who draws upon the shades of **Rubies** and **Sapphire**

Endowed with the Beauty of Cleopatra

and the Jewels of Alexandria

To create something so beautiful,

filled with such deep emotions

Like roses of cherry blossoms,

or the sun of a sunflower

These are the temperaments on the canvas

That is rich in deep **Crimson**

and is royal as **Violet**

Filled with the effervescent of lavender

and as **Brown** as a clay pot

These are my temperaments

created for my pleasure

Filled with moods none can fathom

As dark as a **Black** licorice,

or as bright as a sunset

These are the moods that will never wither,

from a temperament of a blank canvas

They will grow as blades of grass

seeking wisdom from those who will answer

Nourishing my very thought process with colors from a rainbow

Never would I have imagine the creation of my temperament

That goes beyond the absents of color

and reaches towards a blank canvas

As gentle as a **White** *crane on a summer's day*

or as hard as a cypress tree shaped in an origami

These are the axis beyond my spectrum –

Deep within the crevices of my consciousness

Filled with such passion and ever growing madness

While being obsessed with a never waking slumber

To create something from my temperament

That exudes the essence of my spirit

and goes beyond the realms of my comprehension

To a place called, **"Imagination"**

109

That's filled with the endless wonders of creation

Representing the colors of my temperament

As *Green* as a Lily-pad, or as *Orange* as a salamander

Filled with the essence of *White* lotuses

and the passion of blissfulness

That reaps the soul of the wind

and caresses the edge of the fabric

Creating something so majestic and innocent

From a life breathing being the soul of eternity

That goes beyond the wings of ether

and encompasses my eternal aura

To create a picture called, **"Emotion"**

Coming from the temperament of a bl___k canvas

THE ROAD TO RECOVERY

After realizing my lie, I am now trying to find my place in the world. I am looking at myself in a new light. I am trying my best to move forward. After being diagnosis with schizophrenia, my emotions have been turbulent. The reason I have been uneasy is because part of me doesn't want to believe the diagnosis. I have been through so much in my life. My family has been extremely supportive. It is time for me to once again step into uncharted territory. I would be lying if I didn't say I wasn't afraid. All the things I had went through has prepared me for this moment. The truth within me is growing. Now is the time for me to step out of my comfort zone. I went through a life threatening situation involving the reduction of my medication.

The first time I tried to reduce my medicine I ended up in level one ICU. My mom was with me through that entire experience. I was unconscious and didn't know what was going on. I ended up having neuroleptic malignant syndrome (NMS). My vitals were all over the place. It was only by the grace of God that I was able to pull through that event. While facing sheer adversity in my own life, I have learned to appreciate the little things. I am now preparing myself to reduce my medication once again. Only this time I will have more support.

I always felt alone in the past, but it feels different now. The people I have in my life care about my well being. I am not alone. It is difficult for me to see the positive. I have felt alone and isolated for years. I have done numerous things to prepare for the reduction. First, I went Vegan and added some supplements to my diet. Later on, I switched from being Vegan to being Paleo and try to get plenty of rest, so my body and mind is in peak condition. This journey has been unique, but I would not trade it for the world. Getting to know me has been a life changing experience. I was a stranger and didn't know anyone including myself. I am the author who has a special heart. Who cares about people. Who wants the best for me and my family. The role I play is to trust the Lord. I know it will be difficult, but He is with me. No matter what happens I know the Lord will have the last word.

Corridor

The dust has settle as we walk the road

We see something and then nothing

A mirage

The piercing of ones heart who searcheth for Thee

We take a step and a step

Leaving what was left of me

To see what has never been seen

The scene changes

Our surroundings have deepened

The feeling of liberty

I know this place...I know this place

Who am I?

The one who was lost but now is found

As we walk the path

Moving to and fro

Searching

Finding and introspecting

Drawing closer

Ever nigher

To Thee

Restoring me

This journey I have been on has been a difficult one. The road was everything but straight. It had dips, curves, heights, and lows. I guess that is what you call life. Unfortunately, my road was tattered and needed to be repaired. I have been looking for the straight and narrow gate with an aging road. I am on a journey of self discovery and healing. The pathway shows character and longevity. I walk this road never leaving the pavement, while looking at the changing scene. I never thought about where this road was taking me until now. The journey of ones life is something we all uniquely travel. We may not be in control of things on this road, but that is what make this journey fascinating. The best part of all this is that there is another set of foot prints walking along side of me. No matter what the outcome maybe, I know in my heart that I have recovered what I had lost and no one will take that away from me. My thoughts have been all over the place. I feel like the Lord has handed me His business card and it feels so heavy. How can one person bare the weight of God when He has handed you a blessing in such a small package? God doesn't have to hand you a physical object in order for you to realize the weight load that is being carried. The pressures I have received in my life has revealed my psi (pounds per square inch) level. I have been struggling trying to figure out what God wants me to do in my life. How does my mental break coincide with His plans for me? I guess I should stop wasting my time worrying about how my journey is going and just try my best to appreciate the moment.

The day was long and time was short. I was flying by the seat of my pants, realizing the importance of opening up my eyes. I am alive. The sign of a free thinker. There I was alone in the room, contemplating on what to do. I never knew it would be this way as I was screaming for relief. Recovery...what does this mean? Recapturing what I had lost? It is hard to imagine. I was seeing and feeling things that were false. Do I accept my condition as truth, or consider it to be a lie? What is real or fake? It was real to me. I am doing my best to keep my mind open to the possibilities. How can any sane person think to do such a thing to another without considering all possibilities? How can I make a decision under these circumstances? I am wedged between two forces. The lie and the truth. Who will prevail? I am labeled mentally ill.

Where to begin? There are so many things that has happened to me during my initial experience of being called mentally ill; frightening experiences. Let me be real with you for a moment. I have gone through so many things in my life, it is sometimes difficult to see the light at the end of a tunnel.

I am still upset with how my life has turned out in spite of the assistance from the hospital and my family. I am angry, and this anger has caused me to have tunnel vision. I am angry with my diagnosis, my parents, and myself. I am tired of being abuse by people who never receive my wrath. I have to remind myself and reexamine my motives as to why I do or say things in regards to my feelings. The source of my motives have derived from emotional pain. I have struggled with this stimulus for a very long time. It is hard to deal with these emotions caused by the events in my past. I am human. My motives are not always pure, but it is hard to look at oneself in those difficult moments. I am so tired.

The year I had my break was the year of hell for me. We were constantly running in the beginning of my journey by day and I was having disturbing dreams at night. I was even scared to be alone most of the time because I did not know what was going on with me. The terror I once had was real. Who am I to hold such credence to the fact that these types of events could happen to me, or to anyone else for that matter. I have to be honest with you and myself. I am having a really hard time accepting the truth when it comes to my medical condition. I have been distracted, manipulated, and even patronized to the point of accepting my situation as being true. I want it to be a lie and wake up from this living nightmare. Is this a dream or really bad practical joke?

This journey we are on is not for the faint of heart. It takes real courage to step out and "Live" each and everyday. My diagnosis has recently been changed from schizophrenia to post-traumatic-stress-disorder (PTSD). At this point, it does not matter to me what the diagnosis is. The care I have received from everyone involved has been appalling. I know that I need to advocate for myself better, but I am so tired.

Right now I don't know what I want to do with my medication. I have mix feelings. I am scared. I had lost control last time and the whole experience ways heavily on my mind. Even after I reduce from my medicine, I may have to live with this condition. What will be the outcome of me? The thought of reducing will make anyone think twice. Ultimately, the decision is mine and I think that is what scares me the most. I just don't know what to do. Go or stay...fight or flight. I have been trying to sort out my feelings. I am doing my best to try and way in the pros and cons, but there are still so many things I just don't know. What are the lesser of two evils? Is there a way out? What does recovery mean for me? I just don't know.

I have finally reached my decision. I have decided not to reduce my medication. I just needed sometime to think about the ramification of getting off the medicine. I don't respond well to change, especially when I don't know what caused my condition. It is just too risky. It is not easy. I have no intentions of gambling on my life over things that are beyond my control.

I guess this is the part where faith comes into play. I am trying not to trust my own judgment. I am moving forward with my past behind me. The word, "Trust" doesn't comes easy for me because that mean letting go of self. I know this will be difficult. We all like to be in control of our circumstances, but our lives are not our own. They belong to the Lord who love us deeply. I know this experience was dramatic, but I was going down the wrong road. It was desolate and lifeless. A barren wasteland leading towards a dead end. The Lord wants something better for me. I am trying to lean on His words of promise. I am currently trying to find that spark of hope that the Lord is leading me towards recovery. He has given me a new view on life.

A NEW PERSPECTIVE

I have a new perspective on life. For individuals who have made a transition in their lives, change can be difficult for the people around them to accept. The people who are close to you only see the old you, instead of embracing the transformation. I know for some people letting go of the past can be a challenge, but it is not fair to the person who has made an effort in wanting to better themselves and change. I bet you are asking yourself what will happen next? Will I be strong enough to handle these changes? I don't know if I have the strength. You are doubting whether you can overcome this problem and are scared. You are not alone. You can succeed. I started thinking about things involving my circumstances, and began to wonder what was missing in my life? What defines me as a person? How do people's reactions affect my belief system? Do the ends justify the means? The road I have created for myself is not clear. There are still people in my life who are still healing from their wounds which I have inflicted. The important thing is to connect with people. One day you may find yourself standing in a room alone wondering where everyone has gone. It is important to be true to one self when it comes to being healed. Ask questions about yourself. What does it mean to be healed? When people say, "I am healed," are they talking about a spiritual or physical healing? Spiritual healing can take place when people see how God views them in each other. This mentality can manifest itself in the hearts and minds of people. Every moment with each other brings about a new beginning. This process is more than just about you feeling good. It is about realizing that you are special and that being different is not a bad thing. I am learning everyday what God's love means to me. God has given us the ministry of reconciliation that we help others let go of the burdens that they have carried in their lives by seeing the truth.

Now all things are of God, who has reconciled us to Himself through Jesus Christ, and has given us the ministry of reconciliation (2 Corinthian 5:18 KJV).

There is a dream I want to accomplish. I want to help others live their lives in truth. I am not saying that people are living a lie, because I don't have the right to say such things, but I want people to live their lives to the fullest. The only person who knows whether he is living a lie is the individual. The mindset of individuals are constantly changing in the world of introspection. How can we envision this world through the lens of our limited minds? The truth is that no one can really judge the heart except for God.

There are times where being a non-conformist can be a good thing, because there is nothing wrong with thinking outside the box, or not accepting what society deems to be normal. As a writer I am constantly fighting against the grain when it comes to my viewpoints. There is nothing wrong with being an individual. It is beneficial to have a moral center and continue to live in truth. I can't help but wonder, is it really worth living a lie? No! There are so many people out there who are doing things that are against the norm of what society deems to be unacceptable. I don't know what to say to those individuals. I pray that they will see the light. Furthermore, to mislead others as criminals in order to further ones own agenda is beyond truth.

The concept of truth and lies is woven deep within the fabric of our makeup and realizing this can lead to a greater understanding of each other.

Humans have the capacity to reach some level of understanding, but only if we choose to do so. The power of choice. Free will is something of a enigma, yet it is directly connected to truth and lies. The power to believe a lie or to tell the truth. What we choose in life has a direct correlation to these two entities. You can't control these two forces, nor can you mitigate their existence. They are too intricately involve in our lives and because of this we have been granted a gift that is often times taken for granted.

Free Will

As these powers collide between

Light   *and*   Darkness

Who can perceive these two forces of

Good   *and*   Evil

Who can cast the veil between

Life   *and*   Death

And embrace the fabric of

Order   *and*   Chaos

Through the depths of

Creation   *and*   Destruction

Beyond the realms of

Heaven   *and*   Hell

Where my emotions are kept secret
From the ever waking world
Through the core of my being are my...

Friends   *and my*   Enemies

Where the...

Spirit   *and the*   Flesh

Clash; beyond the realms of

Peace   *and*   War

Where the depths of humanity; dwells
Through the act of the

Beginning   *and the*   End

That pierces through my very flesh
And touches every facet of my body
Through these two forces of

Love   *and*   Hatred

Lies the depths of...

Salvation   *and*   Damnation

Where the essence of

Truth   *and*   Lies

Dwells
Deep within the depths of this mortal shell
Where truth be told
Lies misleads
Gates abound
SHUT
I can never go back
It is not fruitful to be known or seen
By ones own reflection to me
For this is the key to your salvation

To choose between...

God   and   Man

For this is a celestial rebirth
That encompasses our mortal flesh
Through the act of our sacred atonement
And the power to choose between

Light   and   Darkness

What door have you opened and what door have you closed? There are doors people choose everyday and each one can represent a truth or a lie. We enter the room with a key and unlock the answers or mysteries of what we consider to be important or painful to us, while trying our best to interpret everything and figure out what truth or lie dwells within. I had locked myself away in my own lie. Let go of the lie and unlock the truth. People need to be careful with what they expose their soul's to on a regular bases. The brain is such a powerful organ, but only if the gatekeepers remain intact. The gatekeepers to the mind are the nose, mouth, ears, eyes, and flesh. Lets imagine if one or even two of these gatekeepers were compromised in some way. What would the world be like if we started seeing, or experiencing things that went beyond our normal senses? How would we interpret the experience? How would we live under those types of conditions? The

125

experienced I had attacked the gatekeeper of sight, the gatekeeper of hearing, and the gatekeeper of touch. What we often ingest become a part of us in our everyday lives, which is why we must be careful about what we consume on a regular bases. You hold the key that guides your destiny and the keyhole that allows the essence of truth and/or lies to flow right through your very being.

I sometimes wonder, what was in the fruit that Adam and Eve consumed from the tree of knowledge of good and evil? What was the content, and how could one act produce such a devastating effect? This is only a theory so bear with me, but I believe that it contained the essence of truth and lies. The digestion of both truth and lies also introduced death. This would include sin, which is an enemy against God. The source of this transgression was produced by a lie. The very first lie believed and ingested by humanity that became woven deep within the fabric of our makeup. I believe in this war of gestation in regards to how we view ourselves, or each other, and how we interpret things through the lens of this world. The carnality of this event has produced confusion, misunderstandings, strife, and wars among humanity. The beauty behind this event is that it has also produced the concept of redemptive love. The price that was paid for all to see and believe through blood, sweat, tears, and sacrifice that the Lord had shed on that faithful day. Christ was able to ignore the lies that was being produced by Satan in the Garden of Gethsemane and revealed the truth of His redeeming love for all of us. There is a difference between conditional and unconditional love. As humans we often times want something more in return for the love that we give or receive. We sometimes place stipulations on that love, especially if the person's heart was broken. I guess you can say that it is a defense mechanism caused by things we have learned over the coarse of our lifetime. The person is afraid of getting hurt for one reason or another. Unfortunately, this is not what true love is in its truest of form. The beauty of unconditional love is that it requires no strings attach to it in order for a person to receive it. I feel like that it is important to define what true love is for oneself and the beauty behind it. It is one of the many treasures and mystery that captures the hearts and minds of humanity.

What is the love of God and how does one obtain it? It isn't something that you can earn. It is freely given to anyone who wants to receive it. I don't have all the answers to this subject, but sometimes it makes you want to think about life in a different way; like the miracles of waking up each and everyday. This period of time has given me a unique opportunity to look deep within myself. How does this knowledge produce a change within us, because every thought life has its own genesis. The beginning of every thought is cultivated within the mind, and it ends with revelation. This reveals not only the truth and/or lies within our minds, but also the source of where it all begins. The fruit of our thoughts are being produced every single day. The mind is where the Spirit of God resides. Who can contemplate the vastness and totality of its complexity? The synapses...the neurons...the structure through which we think...right down to our very own nervous system. The mind is without form or shape until you hear these words, "Let there be..." deep within the crevices of your consciousness. The heart and mind are symbiotically dancing with each other in a synergistic like waltz. The mind is where the information is being gathered and with that knowledge comes the power of choice. The heart is where the passion and drive is being motivated by the thoughts within our minds. These symbolic entities are interconnected with each other and function as a conduit to our very most inner being. The mind has many rooms within itself that needs to be cleaned out. One of those rooms reside in our own neighborhoods.

There are individuals out in the world who have made a difference in helping our communities to be better, but they are few and far in between. I wish they were next door to me, so I can say, "Hello neighbor." What lie dwells in our communities? There are so many facets of people who have benefited from the conditions of our poverty stricken neighborhoods. The people in these communities have lost more than they can stomach. When I look outside I see possibilities, but I also see conflict and I am wondering what happened? Understanding the community's history is the first step, because the lies of the past can often determine someone's future. Know that truth and lie will be widespread over years of development or neglect. Healing the people will heal the neighborhood. For people to heal a neighborhood, it will be necessary for them to take on new and diverse roles.

Life is like a narrative in a play with a protagonist and antagonist. The role a person can play switches from day to day. Depending on how the person views his life will often times define a truth or lie. We all try to discover our purpose in life and the only way anyone can do that is by living it, but it can be difficult if the person is constantly looking back instead of moving forward. Allow Jesus Christ to show you the way. What you perceive within yourself will project outside yourself. We go through life with many ups and downs that we often overlook things that make life worth living. God has weathered me through the storms of life. I can say from experience that I didn't like living a lie. We forget that there are people out there who care about what we say or think. Anyway, I want to share what I know. The more we fill that void caused by the removal of lies with truth, the more it becomes easier to see how special we are. Hopefully, this will produce healing. Having a relationship with God out of love and not fear has shown me that it is important to the healing process. I am special and so are you. The waves of life will finally calm and the lies will become more distance. One of the hardest things about life is living through the good and the bad. When life throws us a curve ball, we hope that it is leading us to something better. Life has many pathways to choose from. Once chosen it can be difficult to determine which way it is going. Is it traveling towards a lie or a truth?

The best way to see where your path is going, is to see where your path has been. The directions of one's life is not predetermined by others, it is defined by you and the choices you make. You have encountered a fork in the road and need to choose which way to go. Your journey has been a long one. A compass of truth guides people in the right direction and that requires faith without which it (faith) is impossible to know which way to go. What direction will you take north, south, east, or west? Truth can lead you down a path of great surprises. For me, as I stated earlier, it was the knowledge that I was not alone and God truly existed and cared about me. For you it could be that you are a good person with a lot to offer. Remember that the goal is to keep moving forward. People

131

need to learn how to let go of what was, so they can embrace on what is, and imagine of what things to come. You can't dream about tomorrow if you are constantly worried about today. When you meet resistance, it is better to create a new path under God's guidance and see where that will lead. God has the final say in all situations so *"Never Give Up,"* Artist Yolanda Adams.

Inner World

I guess there are still unresolved feelings in my heart, but there is a lot of

pain

The scars are deep caused by various people

I have feelings...I have feelings too

The feelings I have are crushed into so many pieces

Scattered Emotions

I pick up one piece and it hurts

I feel the stings of the past

The work is long and hard, but it has to be done

I create a new picture...oops

Crushed Dreams

A new set of pieces fall to the ground

I look at the mess and give a sigh

As I pick up one piece they feel heavier and heavier

The longer the work progresses the harder it is to complete

I create a masterpiece

The work is finally done...breathe

I get things to protect it

Weapons

Only to no prevail I feel rain from nowhere

I look behind me, and my piece begins to melt

I am in shock, and scream NOO!!!

I scramble to save the piece, but it is an uphill battle

Ruin

I look around wondering what had happened

Where is this opposition coming from

Regardless of how many times I have created the picture

My work will be done with God's help

Hope

And we desire that everyone of you do shew the same diligence to the full assurance of hope unto the end (Hebrew 6:11).

I could never have known such mercy the Lord had shown me. I can never understand the depth of His love or my sorrow. The tears I shed during my weakness. The pain ensnared me. I was swallowed up by my own grief not knowing what will happen next. My world was a place of darkness. The hues that saturated my existence were fading. I wanted to be loved by those closest to me. The void that was created and the lie that was formed nearly consumed me. My life started off as a scared little boy, and I became a man whose feelings were closed. I felt indifferent to my circumstances, I didn't care. Those times I felt alone and safe in my breakable shell. I didn't want to feel the pain until I grew numb. It was too much to bear. The depth of my heart became icy cold. My soul cried out the utterance of a sorrowful man. My dreams were being twisted and tormented by a person with no name or face. Please someone, I begged, "Show Mercy!" as I desperately tried to endure my trial. I was on my knees crying out for help. Please heavenly Father heal my aching heart. I am a sinner and I need your help. I looked up only to have ashes fall from a blacken celestial being from an unknown source - a product of a broken spirit. A mound of ashes has formed the final result of the old me. I looked around the pile and found a beautiful empty box with a icy heart next to it. The box represented the essence of me. The icy heart portrayed my emotions - a lack of empathy. These objects of gifts are ashes and a heart which were wrapped up by things unwanted. A glorious light of mercy revealed the truth on these entities. The light is a representation of mercy being shined on the ash, the box, and the heart. The illumined heart begins to melt by the warmth of the light - it is finally free. The frozen valley has been lifted from an icy prison. As I stared at these objects, I thought I had sealed these things within me. These elements that have laid before me continued like precious jewels in my life. I held on to what anguished me the most, feeling empty inside. The Lord saw my pain and wanted to mend it. I asked the Lord for a, "*Depth of Mercy*," Artist: Selah.

Thy sun shall no more go down; neither shall thy moon withdraw itself: for the Lord shall be thine everlasting light, and the days of thy mourning shall be ended (Isaiah 60:20).

I am in the process of healing also. I have tried to do my best to take the high road when it comes to my experiences, but I will eventually reach my destination and hopefully it will be at a place where I can be happy. The Bible is an excellent source of discovering truth, use it and apply it to everyday life. The Mind of God from the beginning to the end. It is a book of hope that is used to better our lives. I am not the only one who needs to be healed so maybe this book will help someone fill a space in his heart where a void was created. Everyone has a message. It may not be the same, but everyone has one, so what is yours? What is your story? Each one of us has a small voice inside. This sound guides and protects us when we need it the most. I am fortunate to have such an awesome experience, and know that God has been leading me. I am in good company. Of all the people He has helped through the ages, he decided to help me. The challenges I have faced have given me a unique testimony.

I feel like things are coming full circle. I say this because when I was little I had a dream of being attacked by something bad. All of sudden, the dream changed and I was surrounded by light and it was peaceful. God has a interesting way of communicating to you when He wants your attention,

"When The Saints Go To Worship," Artist: Donald Lawrence & The Tri-City Singer.

As I am listening to the music, images of people flood my mind. They are individuals who I have encountered in my past. The last face I see is me. All of sudden, the scene changes and those faces are lined up on my left and right. They represent people who had hurt me and they don't speak a word. I begin to walk in between them and in the distance I see this person walking towards me. We finally meet and the person is me when I was little holding a teddy bear. The little me looks up and I look down. We begin to hug each other and then a huge door surrounded by light appears. The door is as big as a skyscraper and it is translucent. We walk towards the door. All of sudden, fire appears and surrounds us, but it is put out. I open the door and we are surrounded by light and it feels peaceful. The difference is that I am not alone. There are people here who have cared and protected us. I am not the only one who the Father is trying to invite into His present. God wants to welcome everyone including you into the sanctuary. All you have to do is accept the invitation.

Lift up your heads, O ye gates; and be ye lift up,

everlasting doors; and the King of glory shall come in (Psalms

24:7).

I just want to say that it has been a pleasure leading you down a path that will help you achieve healing. I encourage you to seek the Lord. God is waiting on us and wants to comfort us in our pain. The Lord redeem me back to Him. I tried my best to run away from myself, but it was not possible. I needed to wake up from my slumber after emotionally crying out. I needed help from the Lord. I deceived myself thinking that loneliness was something to cherish. I was blind to what I was doing and feeling that He needed to wake me up. My tears were as full as the ocean deep only I could not see the bottom. The Lord pulled me from the abyss back into the light. I was drowning and didn't have the strength to float on my own. The Father is calling each person to form a true relationship with Him. Don't let the lies of the past consume you. We all have truth and lies within each of us. It is up to us whether we reject the lie or accept the truth. The battle of your belief system starts in the mind – a war between lie and truth. As humans we are caught in the middle of the ebbs and flows of stability and chaos not realizing how our actions will affect us or others. As the essence of my heart washes on to shore, the war of my faith wages on between truth and lies. Which one will I choose to believe in? Which one will prevail in my heart? I ask you to look deep within yourself to discover what you truly believe. The only person who is stopping you is...

The Lord has written the fruit of His Spirit on my heart. He has given me the greatest attribute that I have been searching for in a long time and that is love. It is important not to forget the people who have helped you along your journey. It easy for us to loose site of that. God has shown me my true purpose in life and that is to help others recover what they have lost and to realize that the truth that lies within one self can be revealed. Lie or truth, which one will you choose? God Bless... "*Till I Met You*," Artist: Laura Story

Prayer of The Heart

I ask the Lord in prayer to expose the lies of the heart

within the person who is suffering and grant them peace of mind. You are not alone in your pain. I ask the Lord to reveal within us the truth and grant us access to a new perspective in our lives. I ask the Spirit of Truth to speak to our hearts and give us a contrite like spirit of repentance. Please continue to guide us as we step into a new life with Christ and have peace in our sanctuary. This is my prayer in Jesus name...

Amen

Redemption

With every breath I take

You've allowed me to enter into a secret place

Where You reside

Holy and acceptable unto your Divine

Who can describe?

This inner voice inside

Who gives me eternal life

Through His Son Jesus Christ

Who reclaimed my life

All He wants is to be glorified

For He made the ultimate sacrifice

Giving me the gift of life

Truly is a sight of the glory inside

Secured in the Body of Christ

Whether it be Jew or Gentile

Believing on the Word of God

Hallelujah

END

Thank you for reading, "The Truth That Lies Within." I hope it has been a blessing for you as it has been for me. I look forward to hearing your thoughts on the book.

About Author

Jonathan Marte' has been through a dramatic experience. He has learned an important lesson that can only come from God. He is not alone. This was a huge revelation for him. The many issues that he faced has given him a new perspective on life. He wants to use what the Lord has taught him to help others through his writing and poetry. The song selections helped him through some difficult times. He encourages you to seek them out. They opened up his heart after carrying such a heavy burden. The purpose of this book is to recover from the pains of the past in order to see a brighter future.

www.ingramcontent.com/pod-product-compliance
Lightning Source LLC
Chambersburg PA
CBHW020501030426
42337CB00011B/183